& THERE SHE GOES

HER WAY

Josi Dumont

About the Author

Josi Dumont is an ICF Certified and Accredited Leadership & Mindset Coach and holds a Diploma of Higher Education in Economics & Management. Before starting her coaching career, she spent almost a decade at a Fortune 500 company where she worked her way up to Senior Finance Professional, Product Owner, and Global Project Lead.

As she moved across countries, Josi started studying intensively how to become your best self through mindset and leadership. Her passion led her to be part of several design teams tasked to restructure the department according to the Agile Methodologies and New Ways of Working.

Despite her steep career, Josi experienced burnout and was forced to make drastic decisions for herself and her life. She then decided to take the leap and follow her souls calling to become a coach. It is her mission to help as many women as possible to learn to trust themselves fully and lead a life and business they love, so they can have the impact they seek to make this world a better place, their way.

Content

Introduction

The fact that you are holding this book in your hands right now is no coincidence. Yup, you read that right.

If you are reading these lines right now, then it is because this book was supposed to find its way to you, and I would love to invite you to dive deeper into these powerful pages to learn *why* you were destined to be here at this moment. By reading this book, you may learn something about yourself that you never noticed before; you may unlock something within yourself that you didn't believe was there or possible; you may even find yourself ignited by these pages, ready to shine your light in its fullest magnificence.

This is my intention for this book. This book is for the woman who is done playing small. It is for the woman who wants to take control over her life and walk the talk with purpose, conviction, confidence, and utter self-belief. It is for the woman who is ready to wave goodbye to Imposter Syndrome, self-doubt, worry, procrastination, or whatever else it is that keeps her feeling small. It is for the woman who wants to welcome the good shit into her life and be prepared for when the bad shit hits the fan. This book is for the woman who wants to live life her way, who wants to just be herself and feel safe doing so. This book is for you.

All of these might be big promises to make for one book. So, my second invitation here is to throw the impossibilities out of the window, right now. Because all of this is absolutely possible for you. The conditions? No room for excuses, no room for doubt, and all of the space for believing and knowing that your life can change, too.

Otherwise, you wouldn't be holding this book in your hands right now. This is tangible proof that you can do it. Because I herewith asked the universe to send this book to all of the women who want more and who are utterly capable of creating their dream lives. And here we are!

You might wonder, *"Why do you care? Why do you care if I live my life to the max or not?"* And to that I say, *"I do care deeply because I am on a mission to uplift and empower as many women as possible to be their best and most authentic selves. Because I know it will make this world a better place."* Think about it: if every woman fully loved and accepted herself, there would not be any behind-the-back gossip, jealousy, and tearing down of one another. Instead, there will be compassion, support, empowerment, and a deep connection and understanding of how incredible each and every one of us are.

If every woman could be fully confident in herself and use her potential to the fullest, there would not be a need to compare ourselves to others and wonder who is better or worse. Instead, there would be full focus on your own life, healthy boundaries that protect your peace, and genuine admiration from peers whilst we all collectively lift each other up.

If every woman lived her life her own way and put herself first, there would not be a one-size-fits-all world, rather diversity and individuality would be even more celebrated, and there would be no more fear of judgement because every woman will be living her life however it makes her happiest. This may sound idealistic, but I believe that it's possible, and it starts with you.

There is no better time than now for women to step into their empowered selves.

We have come a long way already, but we are not yet done. There are many more gifts, like yours, that need to be shared with this world. There is so much more potential that can be unlocked. There is so much more happiness that can be created.

And your time to take part in this has come. It starts right now and here. And with this I have a third invitation for you, before you continue reading. Set yourself an intention right now by answering these questions for if you were to unlock your best version of yourself:

- *What would be possible?*
- *What would you make real?*
- *What would you stand for?*

Write down whatever comes up for you and promise to yourself to uncover and to start evolving into this version.

Because this version is already within you; it has always been. It never left; it doesn't need to be created or trained. You already are this version of yourself. Believe it, know it, be it.

This book will help you pull apart the layers of the "onion" that cover up and keep that version of you hidden. It will shed light on things that you might not want to be uncovered. But, here's the thing: the best version of yourself isn't afraid of holding up the mirror. On the contrary, she knows how to embrace it, acknowledge it, and reap the benefits of doing so. You will also activate your inner strengths and learn how to use them to your advantage; you will find yourself sticking to the good habits you always wanted to include in your routine (like going for a walk first thing in the morning, meditating every day, drinking more water, cutting out sugar, exercising, painting, puzzling, journaling, reading before bed. Whatever it is you will learn how and enjoy sticking to them rather than putting them off for a future that never seems to come). You will learn to embody this "new" best version of yourself and push the green button that will change your life.

To help you with this, each chapter in this book consists of a powerful combination of examples from empowered women, including myself, so that you have more and more proof of what is possible for you, too. I've also included specific exercises that will help you to change your life as you read and get the most out of this book.

I highly recommend not rushing through this book. Read the chapter, do the exercise, observe, experiment, and adapt. You have full control over what and how you do the exercises in this book or how you adopt the wisdom shared in these pages. You also have full control over the impact these will have on you. The more open you are, the more you can make it work for you, and the better and greater the results will be that you reap. If there's anything that doesn't resonate, don't get hung up on it. Leave it for a bit, let it marinate in your subconscious and come back to it later. This book is not me telling you exactly what to do; it is more of a collection of things that have worked for me and others, and you are free to choose what works for you. Take what resonates, leave what doesn't. This is your first exercise in trusting yourself, babe.

If you do find yourself resisting the exercises, questions, or words at times, don't be disheartened. Instead, be curious. What exactly are you resisting here? Is it a fear? If yes, I will show you how to work through this, too. If it is a genuine call from your intuition informing you that a specific chapter isn't right for you at the moment, mark the page and move onto the next one. Come back to it once you have worked through the rest, because perhaps you needed to learn or uncover something else first. Whilst this book is intended to be read in order, I want to make clear that this is my way, but it doesn't have to be your way of getting the most out of this book. So again, whatever works best for you is what you must do.

I've also prepared some amazing accompanying resources for this book. On the respective page, you can find a link or footnote to the resource. These vary from meditations to video trainings, worksheets, and more. I also strongly recommend reaching out to me whenever you have questions or if something is unclear; the best ways to do so are via direct message on Instagram @Josi_Dumont or email: josi@josidumont.com. The reason I am doing this is because you are committing to yourself right now and I want to applaud that and support you on that journey as much as possible. This is my commitment to you—my promise as your author, coach, friend, stranger you never met before, yet here you are.

So, with the introduction and explanation done and dusted, let's dive into unlocking your utmost potential—this is going to be great!!!

P.S.: Whilst this book is for women, there is no doubt that men will 100% be able to learn a thing or two as well. So, even if you identify as a male human being and you want to become better today than you were yesterday, this book is for you too.

Section 1:
The Wake-Up Call

Chapter 1: Where You Are Now

You are in control of your life,
stop giving your power away!

In this chapter, you will evaluate your life as it is right now and together, we will hold up the mirror and take a peek at where you are headed, what you do well, what you do not so well, how you long to be different, and what you want to achieve.

Like many, 2020 was the most significant moment in my life. I realised that things in my life went to shit. From the outside looking in, I had the perfect life. A blooming career in Finance with great opportunities and good money, living abroad in a house that was only a 20-minute walk from work, being in a long-term relationship with my first ever boyfriend and about to get married, owning two cats, maintaining a healthy body, and having amazing, supportive friends. What else could I have wanted? How could I be unhappy with all of this in my life?

Let's look at it from the inside, looking out. At my work, I was burning out in the project I was leading and the opportunities in the company weren't aligned with what I wanted. My house was slowly falling apart. My relationship was always very toxic, but my past self ignored the red flags and was ridden by fear of judgement of what others would think. In fact, I initially broke up with my boyfriend back in mid 2020 but gave it one last chance because of all these fears. In doing this, I put myself through hell even longer. Then again, it was a much-needed lesson for me to learn; that's the beauty of hindsight! Plus, I always had everything under control, until then. I kept on wondering, *"How could I possibly have it all fall apart now?"* Additionally, my body was plagued by hormone imbalances, one of my cats broke her leg, and some of my friends turned out to not be in it for the long term. The ones that were, I wouldn't see for years (thanks COVID).

I was at my lowest. It started to dawn on me, yet I was still fighting it. Deep down, I knew that something needed to change. I didn't want life to be and feel this way. I didn't want this. I didn't want to work in Finance any more. I didn't want to be in this relationship any more. I didn't want to live in that house with a garden I never spent time in (which also had too many spiders). Of course, I still wanted my cats and friends, but more than that, I longed to simply be happy again, to feel like I was adding value and making an impact. But, when you're in the troughs, this is way easier said than done.

And so, it still took me working for another couple months in the company. Heck, it even took me to agree to get married and freak out on the wedding day. I kept thinking, *"Please, somebody say no, Please somebody save me!"* But my facade was too strong and no one could tell. No one said no; no saviour was about to rescue me and shout, *"Don't do this, girl!"* Only later I realised that the saviour was there, but it kept quiet... It was me. So instead, I plunged into depression, got agitated easily, shut myself off even more and my husband, now ex-husband, of course, noticed this. He came into my office and asked why I had been so off and distant ever since the wedding. This finally gave me the permission to burst. I couldn't bear to wear this mask any longer and I finally called it quits. I looked up how to annul a wedding and got the process going. I didn't just want a divorce, which would have meant that I had to wait at least a year. I wanted to erase this experience, press backspace and start afresh as soon as possible. I have to say, that I am immensely grateful for my Ex that he agreed to the annulment.

But that wasn't all, at the same point in time, our department at my company was going through restructuring once again. Despite me being heavily involved in the design teams and sprints and co-shaping the new world with my fellow colleagues, this restructure hit me harder than the times before. This was most likely because everything was crashing down on me all at once. My whole life as I knew it was in crumbles.

It is a funny thing when you can still feel grief and sadness over the loss of something you didn't actually like. I learned that this is simply because you have adapted to the pain and the discomfort you are in.

Therefore, it is rather natural to feel this way, even if the situation wasn't good for you at all. And any form of change is scary and hard at first. It takes a while to acclimate to the idea of a different life, to get used to not knowing, to let go of stability and security, even if that safety and security are hurting you.

I had hit rock-bottom. I was mentally, physically, and energetically drained and exhausted. But you know, sometimes you got to sink to the bottom to wake up and push yourself back up again. Which is what I did. This was my personal wake-up call. I needed to start proactively seeking change and taking back responsibility and control over my life and feelings. Being as determined as I am, I decided that this can't be it; things *had* to be better. I took one next best step at a time. (Yes, I am referencing a song from Frozen II (2019), and I haven't even watched the movie, it was in fact a client and dear friend who taught me this reference!)

One of these steps I knew had to involve external support, so I signed up for a mini coaching course that I found through my company. I truly am grateful for one of my managers who signed off on all my training requests up until the time I left, so there wasn't even any negotiation necessary to get it approved. This course included two coaching sessions, which were my first ever touchpoints with coaching. They were a massive help to navigate this unknown and scary space. The lady leading the sessions hugely supported me in seeing things more clearly workwise and in making a better-informed decision, which ended up being to seek temporary refuge in another role in mid-2021. Sometimes, you just need to talk through your pros and cons list with someone to get the clarity you seek or already have inside of you. It's like having a sounding board to bounce ideas, thoughts, and goals back and forth to find what feels right.

Shortly after the second session, my mentor back then was about to become a coach herself and was looking to find more clients. Therefore, we transformed our mentor-mentee relationship into a coach-coachee relationship. She started coaching me, and these sessions were truly life-changing. We dove into the dreams and visions I had for my life and any self-sabotaging beliefs that held me back, which helped me to re-discover my strongest personal values, like freedom, impact, and authenticity. Doing this really unravelled what I actually enjoyed and longed to do and accomplish. It felt like a light bulb was fully switched on after years and years of only flickering. It was as if I got struck by lightning and everything was suddenly crystal clear.

I knew what was holding me back (me, myself and I at your service), and I knew what I wanted: happiness, freedom, and the opportunity to make a difference for others.

Audit Your Life

This is the point where I pause my story and together, we dive into *your* story. Maybe you related to some of the things I have experienced. Maybe you even said, "*Holy shit, I'm going through the exact same thing!*" And dare I say, this is exactly why you are reading this book now, because you are ready to change things up and step into your power and live a life you love again. Since my curtain-drop-moment and the journey that unfolded after, I have met many, many women who have experienced burnout, unfulfilled relationships, gruesome jobs, and more. The reason I'm telling you this is because I want you to know that you are not alone. While no one else will ever experience life as you or I do, as each life is so wonderfully unique, the lessons we must learn along the way are very often of similar nature. I'm telling you this because within this book, you will hear the stories of some remarkable women who have worked through the misery and got out the other end as thriving powerhouses. They claimed amazing job opportunities, stepped into leadership positions, reduced their work time, started side hustles, healed traumas, left the 9-5 lifestyle, kicked the toxic relationships to the curb, created time-freedom based lives, built successful businesses, set strong boundaries to protect their peace, learned to love and trust themselves again; the list is endless.

And the key shift that led to all these amazing achievements was this: all of them learned to take back ownership and leadership over their lives by up-levelling into their next best version of themselves, to trust themselves and let go of the self-doubt. None of them ever looked back.

Now it's your turn. Take some time right now to really be very honest with yourself about your life. Where are you right now? How does it feel to be at this point in your life right now? If you go to this link www.josidumont.com/herway and enter the password "HERWAY", I have prepared several free resources for you, including the following exercise, which you can use to make this a little easier. This exercise is called "The Wheel of Life", and here is how to use it.

Exercise: The Wheel of Life

In this exercise, you have a circle divided into 8 different sections that all represent one part of your life right now. For each area, ask yourself how satisfied you are right now with it on a scale from zero (things are shit) to ten (things are flippin' amazing). This is where it is important that you are really, truly honest. Go with your first instinctive reaction and don't overthink it. What we don't want is for you to slip off into the thought process of: "It's not that bad. In fact, I should make it higher". A ten should be the absolute best-case scenario. Your heart should *sing*. "Not that bad" doesn't sound like singing to me. Instead, it's settling and compromising. Your life should no longer include any compromises that prevent you from being your absolute best and happiest self. If you don't want to use the circle you can also note down the numbers only, but do so somewhere you can refer back to later on.

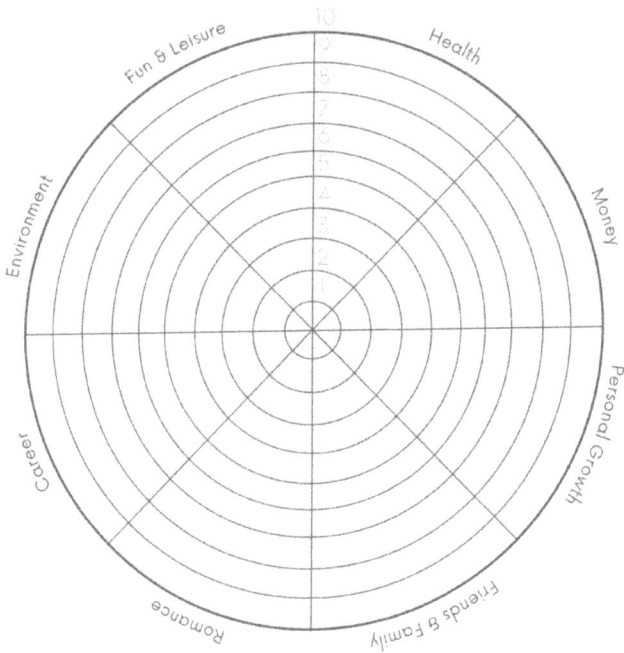

Figure: The Wheel Of Life

As you place your evaluation in each area, you will see the lines form a circle. Below, I put two examples for you showcasing how my wheel of life looked back in 2020-2021 and how it looks right now at the point of writing... It's a huge difference! 2020 looked pretty damn bad. And that's okay if it looks like this for you right now, because this is your wake-up call. This is you shedding light on what you might have ignored for so very long. This is the first step we have to take so that we can change things around. Then, not too long from now, you will have a new rating in your wheel of life. I highly recommend keeping the one you created today, to refer back to and see the phenomenal growth you will have made after today. You will be madly impressed by yourself!

Figure: My WoL from 2020

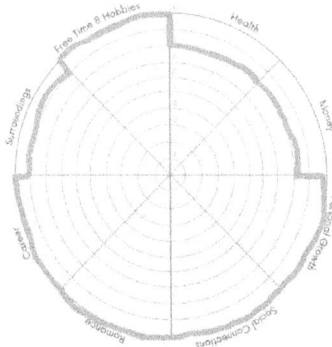

Figure: My new WoL from 2023

Step 1: Complete your Wheel of Life and answer the following questions

After you complete the wheel, take out your journal (or write it on the same paper as the wheel) and ask yourself these questions:

- *Looking at The Wheel of Life, which areas are the lowest for you right now?*

- *Which one of these has the highest priority and importance for you?*

- *Choose one to be your focus for the rest of the time you are reading this book (and possibly beyond if you want to).*

- *How does the current score feel to you?*

- *What is your current reality at this point like?*

Awesome, well done! Before we move on, let's do a quick reset. This is the easiest way to disrupt your current thinking and helps release any negative emotions you might have built up just now whilst auditing and taking a deeper look at your current situation. Which, by the way, is a very normal thing to happen if you are seeking change and experience frustration at how things are right now. In this next step, you will switch gears to start looking forward, and we don't want you to be too engulfed by any negative emotions as you get dreaming. So, we need to get you back into a more neutral space.

You may find more exercises like this sprinkled throughout the book, just to bring you back into a grounded, neutral state. They are great tools to know as well when you might feel anxious or just in general want to snap out of a current way of thinking/feeling. For example, I always do this next breathing exercise before I start a session with a client so that I feel calm, can coach from a place of true connection, and be in the present moment. In this first round, we will focus on your breath.

Breathe deeply into your tummy and chest three times. Hold each breath at the top for a count of four, envision the word "Release" in your mind's eye, then slowly exhale through your mouth. Imagine with each out-breath, you cleanse yourself from any heaviness and negative emotions. This will help you to let go of negative thoughts and emotions. Once you feel a little lighter and more grounded, ask yourself the following questions.

Step 2: Ask yourself these new questions to start dreaming!

- *If the area you chose to focus on (or all areas of the wheel of life) would be at a ten, what would be different?*

- *How would you feel?*

- *What would your day-to-day life look like; what do you enjoy doing?*

- *How are you different from that new version of yourself?*

I understand that this exercise may be tricky. You might respond to them with, "*I don't know.*" If that's the case, simply imagine, use your fantasy, and get dreamy about how life could be.

Then, I want to invite you to dream even further: what would be your cherry on top? What would a twelve or maybe even fifteen look like? What would be possible for you then? Journal out all your answers; you have full permission to dream right now as if you were a young kid again who wanted to be a painter or an astronaut. This is where you get to dream bigger than ever before. Don't you hold back. Go cray cray, my dear! We want #delulu today!

Step 3: Pick your main focus

Choose the area(s) that is (are) most important to you right now, the one(s) that has (have) highest priority at this moment and that you feel drawn to changing the most.

This will be your main focus area for now and we will work together on improving it. I will show you examples from clients and myself of how to raise your score closer to or higher than a ten. You might even find that raising the bar is actually easier than you thought, and you want to add another area to work on. That's totally fine. You are also open to changing your focus completely. But I do urge you to never change it because your self-sabotage type is in control and tells you that it's pointless, too hard, or impossible. There is always a way, and you will find it if you stay committed. I promise.

Once you have finished this exercise, you are ready to move onto the next chapter. Do take your time; there is no need to rush. Oh, and by the way, it's never too late to change your life. You can get married at 60, start a business at 40, travel the world at 50, and start weightlifting at 80. You can do anything at any age. Every person on this planet is on their own timeline, and you are in control of yours alone. The key is to start, so let today be your day one.

Chapter Summary

In this chapter, we explored the importance of no longer living on autopilot, how to properly audit your life, and how to realign it with what really matters to you. The Wheel of Life exercise is a great entry point if you don't know where to start, and it also serves as a progress tracker in x time from now to see how far you have come already. You have now established the areas in life that you want to change and work on. But before we get all excited and our hands dirty, we need to know why what you want isn't your reality yet. And that starts with self-awareness.

Chapter 2: Shedding Light on WTF is Going on

You cannot change what you are not aware of.
Self-awareness is always the first step.

Now that we have identified the gap between your now and where you want to be, we can dive into shedding light on what exactly is preventing you from living life and feeling like a ten. To do so, we will explore your self-sabotage type and practice raising your awareness on where and how it is popping up for you on a daily basis. You might be surprised at first by how much power you let these inner saboteurs have over you!

First things first: what is a self-sabotage type? You may have heard of similar expressions before like saboteur, inner critic, negative inner voice, negativity bias, inner shadow, your monkey brain, mindset blocks, thinking trap, ego-self, or even inner gremlin. They all encompass pretty much the same thing. I call them self-sabotage types and saboteurs because that is their main function: to sabotage you. They are the voices that tell you "*I can't,*" "*I have to,*" or "*I shouldn't*". They restrict you from pursuing your values and going beyond the status quo. They confine you within a box, preventing you from going after your dreams and exploring the possibilities that could bring joy, fulfilment, and aliveness. In short, they want you to stay as you are and not evolve any further. They are highly connected to negative emotions, such as: stress, shame, guilt, sadness, anger, and frustration. The different types even work great together as a team to keep you as small as possible. This is because small equals safe in their eyes. Interestingly, they do that because they care about you, but more on that later. First, we must explore how they come to be.

A saboteur is something that has been created in your childhood. Sometimes, it is a traumatic event. Other times, it's just the subtle comments from parents, guardians, close friends or family and of course, what we are exposed to in the form of society that awaken the saboteurs. It could also be from our own past interpretations of the situation that our brains decided are the truth from that moment on. This means that you don't need to have been traumatised or have had a horrible childhood to create a saboteur. The truth is that even if you were the happiest child on this planet, chances are you still have some form of self-sabotaging behaviour by virtue of being a member of the human society. And I'm not saying this to pick out a flaw. Absolutely not. It just means that you are human.

In fact, the human brain is wired to keep you safe at any point in time—its specialities are in fight, flight, freeze, fawn and trying to make sense of the world around you. In other words, being able to find reason and meaning for something, whether consciously or subconsciously. That's all the saboteurs ever want to do as well; they don't actually mean you any harm.

To explain this even further, let's look at an example from my client Jessica. (*Side note: names, gender and certain other details of clients have been changed throughout this book to ensure utmost confidentiality and anonymity. However, the general story and quotes have been kept the same to preserve these as real-life examples*).

When Jessica first came to me, she wasn't necessarily unhappy. Life was good, she had a job, was married, lived in a beautiful apartment, had great friends, and had just given birth to her son. But, she knew life could be better. While she didn't know exactly how or what she wanted to be better, she was highly invested in personal growth and learning more about herself as well as better using her potential. So, we got to work. We went through The Wheel of Life together and dove deep into it to get clear on where she was presently and where she wanted to be.

The areas that turned out to be the main pain points were her relationship and her job. This is when we further explored her recurring thoughts around her relationship and her feelings. And much to her dismay, a lot was going on there. Jessica was stuck in a thought pattern of people-pleasing, overthinking, and criticising. In terms of her people-pleasing tendencies, she was saying things like, "*Sometimes I will just shut down, retract and not say anything when I'm getting into an argument with my partner because I just want it to stop. I just want it to be harmonious, so I bite my own tongue.*"

When I asked where this might be rooted in or come from, she pondered on that for a moment. She said: "*My parents were fighting a lot and I always wanted to make them happy again. It wasn't like very bad fighting or anything, but it triggered me.*" Despite not being extreme triggers, all these moments in her childhood added up and created Jessica's main self-sabotage type, "the People-Pleaser".

It was a protection mechanism to shield herself from the negative environment and feelings that watching her parents fight caused in her. She was never actually harmed or abused, but just witnessing the arguments caused her brain to tap into fawn mode. This shifted her body into the stress response of trying to please someone to avoid conflict. And it stayed with her throughout all those years.

Our brains love routine and habits, and with repetition, certain behaviours start to run automatically.

As with Jessica's self-sabotaging behaviour, in the form of people-pleasing, which has been well trained over the years as her brain kept returning to this "solution" to keep her "safe". However, as Jessica grew older, this type of behaviour was less and less of actual service to her. On the contrary, it was detrimental to her happiness because she kept putting others before herself. She always ensured everyone else was happy before she looked after herself, if she even ever found time to do so.

The interesting thing about saboteurs is that even though we as humans grow up, get older, and learn, the saboteurs don't. They stay in their child-like state (which is also why the term "gremlin" makes a lot of sense to describe the saboteur). Again, I do want to make it so clear that they in themselves

31

aren't bad. All they want is to keep you safe in the best way they know how. We, as grown-up humans, simply know better the older we get, and notice that their way of doing things is not always the best. The reason I want you to know this is because I often see clients condemning their saboteurs. It's not rare that they would be beating themselves up or judging themselves for having them. Which, you might already have guessed, is another form of self-sabotaging and only leads to a continuation of the vicious cycle. Therefore, the solution to stop self-sabotaging is clearly not self-sabotaging yourself even more, just with a different saboteur. "*But then, what is?*" I hear you ask. Fear not; we will get there.

Before we can start shifting the self-sabotaging behaviour and retrain our brains, it is crucial to know exactly when, where and how the saboteurs come out of their hiding. Similarly to when you are sick, if you only address the symptoms but not the cause, you will never heal. So, we need to shed light on what has caused the saboteur to do its thing, rather than just trying to fire-fight the results. For Jessica it was during fights, but it also showed up at work where she would always allow others to book meetings even in times she didn't want to have any. She would complete some tasks or agree to do something she actually didn't want to do, nor enjoyed doing, but did it for the sake of making others happy. She wanted to keep the peace and prevent arguments from happening (ignoring the fact that it caused an argument within herself and her values).

As you go through the next exercises in this book, you will come to find that saboteurs are everywhere. Imagine you buy a red car, and you absolutely love it. But as time goes on, you notice so many other red cars out there. They are literally *everywhere*. Or, you want to get pregnant and all of a sudden, everyone else around you is popping out babies like crazy. Maybe you fell in love with a new hairstyle and booked an appointment with the hairdresser, only to realise that all of a sudden, everyone has this hairstyle. By the time you sit in the chair, you don't even want it any more. It is the same predicament with our saboteurs. Once you know that they are there, you will find them everywhere, and that's *great* because it shows that your level of self-awareness is already increasing, and we do need to find those little waldos ASAP.

As soon as we find your saboteurs and know where they pop up, the next step is to get clear on what they are actually saying to you, how they feel, and what they make you do or not do. This is where we start healing the root cause of the saboteurs.

For this, it might be helpful to give them two to three minutes of stage time. Think of a recent moment in which you have been hijacked by your saboteur. Maybe you had an amazing new offer idea for your business and got all excited, but then all of a sudden, your doubt kicked in and you started second-guessing yourself, finding all the reasons and excuses as to why this won't work anyway. At that moment, how did you feel? What happened within your body? Were you tense? Did your heart rate go up? What were the exact thoughts you were having? The following list includes some very common examples of thoughts that clients of mine repeat when trapped in self-sabotage mode. Skim through the list to see if any of these resonate but be careful to not adopt them or take them as your truth.

- *"I am not good enough."*

- *"Who do I think I am!?"*

- *"They will hate me if I say no."*

- *"I have to do this, otherwise what are they going to think of me?"*

- *"I don't deserve this."*

- *"I need to work harder to show my worth."*

- *"The more I do, the more valuable I am."*

- *"Looking after myself is selfish."*

- *"Why do these things always happen to me?"*

- *"I can't ever seem to stick to my promises."*

- *"I don't trust myself."*

- *"It's so hard for me."*

- *"I shouldn't speak up; it doesn't change anything anyway."*

- *"Did I use the right tone of voice? Maybe I shouldn't have said that after all."*

- *"I'm so stupid, why did I do that?"*

- *"It's too hard, I will do it tomorrow."*

- *"I have to wait until..."*

Now that you know what your self-sabotage type feels like and hear what it says, give it a name or over-arching description; maybe you even have a picture in your mind that describes them. The clearer you get on how this saboteur shows up for you, the easier it will be for you to notice it from now on. And it can be anything from a strict teacher figure (which is my critic saboteur called Cecile) to mosquitoes, poison ivy, to ghosts and dark clouds. Whatever comes up for you that represents this sensation, go with it.

In case you have some difficulties with this exercise, you can find a link to a free quiz I created to help you to find your top saboteur on the resource page of this book. In addition, you will find a worksheet where you can note down your top four saboteurs so that you have a list you can return to. You may find that you have more than four, or that only one shows up for you right now. That is totally normal. Over time, you can add to the list as each saboteur type has different characteristics. If you decide to take the quiz, you will receive a guide that describes the many types in greater detail. But I will introduce you to them in this book now as well.

The Perfectionist

Origins:

Perfectionism can develop from a combination of high expectations placed on oneself, fear of failure or judgement, and a need for external validation. It may stem from early experiences of receiving conditional love or praise primarily based on achievements, leading to a belief that self-worth is tied to being flawless. It robs your happiness through never feeling good enough and the constant pressure to perform better and keep it up. 80/20 is not an option.

Signs of the Perfectionist:

- You set extremely high standards for yourself and may even hold others to them. You may also experience huge disappointment and become very critical if those are not met.

- You might also spend way longer on a project because you want to get it perfectly right; you don't dare submit anything that's not good enough, and you tend to scratch a whole day off work if you receive any negative feedback and start from ground zero.

- You experience feelings of stress and anxiety if something spontaneous happens that hasn't been planned for or when an unexpected challenge arises.

Example of how this is holding you back:

You had an incredible idea for a new offer to serve your clients and have been working on it relentlessly. However, because

36

you want to get it absolutely perfect before launching, you keep on fine smithing the content, edit the training videos several times, add more worksheets, and maybe even get side-tracked by what others are doing and want to implement that too. Because of this never-ending cycle of creating the most perfect offer, you get in your head and decide it's not good enough and therefore you never launch.

The People-Pleaser

Origins:

The tendency to be a people pleaser often arises from a desire for acceptance, fear of rejection, or a need to avoid conflict. It may be rooted in childhood experiences where individuals learned that prioritising others' needs over their own brought them a sense of safety, harmony, approval, or love.

Signs of the People-Pleaser:

- You often seek approval and validation from others, sometimes even at the expense of your own needs, desires, and well-being.

- You have a hard time saying "no" to other people in the fear of them liking you less and the need to be accepted by them.

- You avoid conflict or confrontation to maintain harmony, even if you must suppress your own feelings and opinions, leading you to feel unsafe expressing your real thoughts and opinions.

<u>Example of how this is holding you back:</u>

You want to create the absolute best experience for your customers and make yourself available for whenever they have questions or need extra support. Sometimes, this might mean that you hop on a call during the evening, even though you already had a long workday. But you fear your clients might think badly of you, or believe you don't care about them, which is why you have a hard time setting boundaries that protect your time and energy.

The Excuse-Finder

<u>Origins:</u>

The habit of finding excuses to avoid or procrastinate on tasks or responsibilities can originate from fear of failure, feelings of inadequacy, or a desire to avoid discomfort or challenges. It may develop as a coping mechanism to protect oneself from potential criticism, failure, or the fear of not meeting high expectations. It is also a stress response in the form of freezing and not being able to act.

<u>Signs of the Excuse-Finder:</u>

- You procrastinate and push out important projects to the last minute, or don't do them at all.

- You find the best excuses not to do something you set out to do, even if it is of long-term benefit for you. Instead, you indulge in short-term pleasure.

- You struggle sticking to habits and tend to finger point others or external situations if something doesn't work out, ignoring your role in the outcomes of your actions or decisions.

Example of how this is holding you back:

It is one of your dreams to become more visible and you would love to collaborate with other business owners to do lives together, come on podcasts, or host a webinar together. One of your business besties has her own podcast and invited you to come on. Despite you wanting to do this so badly, your fear of not being good enough, or not having anything valuable to share, causes you to postpone the interview several times for different reasons. At the same time, you start avoiding chatting to your friends because you feel bad, and end up ghosting her, not further pursuing this opportunity whilst seeing others having great fun and exposure as they come onto the show.

The Victim-Player

Origins:

The victim player mindset can stem from past traumas, experiences of powerlessness, or a learned helplessness. It may result from a belief that external circumstances control one's life. Taking on a victim role can provide a sense of validation and attention or avoid personal responsibility and ownership over one's own life.

Signs of the Victim-Player:

- You think life happens *to* you and that you are a victim of circumstances.

- You hold onto negative past experiences, using them as excuses for current struggles or reasoning as to why you cannot do or change something.

- You frequently complain and express a negative outlook on life, focusing on the unfairness and hardship of it all. You cannot seem to see anything positive come out of a challenge and therefore resist taking ownership or responsibility.

Example of how this is holding you back:

You always wonder how others are so successful with their businesses and make millions in what seems overnight. You feel like you're missing out on a big "secret" they know that has helped them to be successful and you end up subscribing to loads of different coaches and mentors to find out what "it" is. You constantly compare yourself to them, doom-scrolling on social media, wondering why you can't make it work like everyone else, leading you to even consider whether it would be best to just give up and quit.

The Overthinker

Origins:

Overthinking often arises from anxiety, fear, or a need for control. It can stem from a habit of excessive rumination, analysing past events, and worrying about the future.

Overthinkers may tend to focus on worst-case scenarios and struggle with making decisions due to fear of making the wrong choice.

Signs of the Overthinker:

- You spend excessive time lying awake at night going through the events of the day or even further in the past again and again.

- You tend to imagine worst-case scenarios and therefore become more anxious and worry a lot about the future.

- You struggle being present in the moment due to overactive thoughts and rumination.

Example of how this is holding you back:

You received a rather judgemental comment on one of your Instagram posts, criticising your expertise. You can't stop thinking about the comment for days to come. It keeps you awake at night, and you wonder if you maybe would have put some things differently in your post, that that person wouldn't be upset about it. You keep on asking your friends and mentor about it discussing whether to delete the post or comment so others can't see it, and feel like maybe you shouldn't post opinionated posts like this at all any more.

The Analyser

Origins:

The tendency to analyse situations extensively may be rooted in a need for certainty, fear of making mistakes, or a desire to avoid unexpected outcomes. It can result from a cognitive preference for rationality and logic, sometimes leading to over-analysing and difficulties in taking action without extensive analysis.

Signs of the Analyser:

- You experience decision-fatigue due to being stuck in a loop of over-analysing potential outcomes, which can lead to missed opportunities and inability to trust or even use your own intuition.

- You struggle with spontaneous or on-the-spot decision making, even if it is just about the pizza toppings.

- You spend significant time researching or gathering information to make sure you really know all the details before taking action like buying that new bike or which restaurant to go to.

Example of how this is holding you back:

You found an incredible coach that has an amazing Black Friday Offer that you feel like would be perfect for you to tackle your goals and help you to overcome certain challenges in your mindset. But because you have heard from some people that they had bad experiences with a different coach, you are hesitant and feel the need to do loads of research. You look up every detail and go through all possible scenarios in your head, but just can't seem to come to a conclusion. Your gut tells you "*Yes*", but your brain keeps on thinking "*But what if?*" In the end, you don't sign up during the offer, and regret that you didn't make use of it.

The Overdoer

Origins:

The Overdoer mindset can come from a drive for success, validation, or a fear of failure. It may stem from internalised pressure to prove oneself, achieve societal expectations, or overcome feelings of inadequacy. Overdoers often struggle with setting boundaries, prioritising self-care, and fear slowing down or being seen as lazy. They think doing more than less is always better.

Signs of the Overdoer:

- You tend to take on an excessive number of tasks and responsibilities (because otherwise no one else does it or does it right) and you feel overwhelmed and burnt out.

- You tend to neglect your personal boundaries and self-care and experience physical or emotional exhaustion as a result of not allowing yourself to rest.

- You feel guilty or anxious when you are not being productive, and you constantly seek something to do to fill your time instead of laying still and enjoying that pina colada whilst you are on vacation.

43

<u>Example of how this is holding you back:</u>

You are known for always being on the go, being busy and getting stuff done. You are the one, colleagues go to if they need help with certain tasks, and you keep on loading your plate with more things to do. You feel like you can't take time off because of that, as everything would just stand still and turn into an even bigger pile of work when you come back. To prevent that, you secretly work on emails and some "easy" tasks during your holiday, or you play through the next customer call in your mind whilst you're sitting by the pool glancing at the messages in slack. You come back from your vacation, not feeling rested at all, yet you just drink some more coffee and get back to it.

The Critic

(the self-sabotage type that without fail, all of us have)

<u>Origins:</u>

This self-sabotage type often arises from internalised self-judgement, low self-esteem, or a need for control. It may stem from critical messages received during childhood, such as harsh parenting or constant criticism. The inner critic may act as a defence mechanism to prevent disappointment or rejection by pointing out flaws or perceived shortcomings, pushing oneself to constantly work harder or perform better.

<u>Signs of the Critic:</u>

- You are highly self-critical and judgemental of your own actions, appearance or abilities and focus on your flaws and mistakes whilst downplaying any strengths and accomplishments.

- You have difficulty accepting and receiving compliments or praise, feeling uncomfortable or unworthy and simply putting it down as not true.

- You often compare yourself to others and feel inadequate as a result.

Example of how this is holding you back:

Your partner seemed a little quieter lately and you fear that you maybe have done something to upset him/her. You wonder if it is something you said during dinner the other day, or whether you're not attractive any more because you haven't had time to go to the gym lately, or that maybe the sex wasn't that great. You start doubting yourself, and criticising yourself for not being good enough, because you can't even make this one person happy.

As you read through these different self-sabotage types, you may notice that some of them sound similar or you may even think to yourself, *"Holy shit, I got all of them."* This is absolutely normal because in fact, you do have all of them; some are just way stronger than others due to "harder training". They also are great at teaming up and more than one might show up in the same situation. For example, the Excuse-Finder has you procrastinating first and then your Critic comes in and beats you up for it, causing you to feel trapped in an endless downward, negative spiral.

I know that this might be a lot to swallow all at once, so I urge you to put the book aside just for a few minutes, take a couple deep breaths, stretch, or do a mini dance before you continue reading. Or as Professor Lupin would suggest to Harry Potter, have a piece of chocolate; it really helps. Then, when you are ready, here is an exercise to smoke out your self-sabotage types once and for all.

Exercise: Quiz and Saboteur Overview

As described earlier in this chapter, I highly recommend doing the quiz to find out your top self-sabotage type and to then go through the guide or descriptions in this book to really get to know your saboteur. The more you know about them, the easier it is to spot them.

Don't be disheartened; it is totally normal and actually a great sign if you spot them in all sorts of moments and areas of your life. It is proof that you are getting more and more self-aware.

A Note on Self-Awareness

Self-awareness and looking within is an incredibly powerful and often underrated skill to hone. I'm not surprised, since we live in a world where we are flooded with information, sensations, triggers, and influences from the outside on a daily basis. Just open your phone and you can get lost in the depths of the infinite scroll within seconds. In addition, the workplace has fostered such an inhumane work ethic, that we are being conditioned to let go of our humanity and become robots. But also, as a Business Owner, you can easily get swept away by the vast number of tasks to do, client messages to read, and Instagram posts to create.

With all these distractions in the outside world, it's no surprise we struggle finding stillness to go inwards. Talking about emotions, mental health and wellbeing is only really starting to be a topic on the rise. Yet, there is a constant need to be better than everyone else, to continue improving oneself and invest in personal development. However, most people think they do this through learning yet another system, or getting another certification that proves they are experts in accounting. But what they miss is that understanding yourself, and I mean *truly* understanding yourself, is improved through self-awareness. Self-awareness shows you how you handle different situations, how you react, pro-act, how you treat yourself and others, and more.

The amount of times I've heard people say to me "*we don't need this touchy-feely stuff here*", "this is all too woo-woo", or "*being in touch with your emotions is like showing weakness*", is mind-blowing to me. The cherry-on-top statement, that made me cringe and my fingernails tingle was: "*Emotions make for a bad CEO*", which is simply put bullshit. Yes, you should not necessarily make decisions from a place of deep frustration or blind bliss, but this statement simply generalises emotions in general, whilst they can carry valuable messages for you. Though we will dive into this later. Anyhow, what these statements also show me is this: they're most often too scared to go there because of what they might find. They are so under control of their saboteurs, that they close themselves off to the learnings that reside within them. They put a stamp on it and say, "*Vulnerability is bad.*" I'm not the first person to say: *"Actually, it's one of the biggest strengths there is!"* Especially in a world where truly looking inward is often shamed. Continuing to do so to grow and be a better person is an incredibly brave act, and therefore a strength.

I promise you that there is no self-help book out there that would not bang on the fact that you got to be more self-aware if you want to grow. But very often, people like to read over those chapters and don't get the message because they want the quick wins and actions steps, that they can implement right now and see as-fast-as-possible results. The problem with this tactic though is, that you no action will get you anywhere if the setting isn't right. Imagine driving a car towards Disney Land, but you don't put the right destination into the settings, or don't change the language from French to English. You can do as much driving as you want; without the right settings you will not get there.

If you want to be a better human being (or insert anything you want to get better at), you need to shed light on where you are right now and how you are leading yourself.

You need to look inwards, and that's what self-awareness is all about. It's the awakening to your true self, and one of the least woo-woo things out there if you ask me. It's simply put, knowing how you tick. When you know how you tick, you can see what ticks well and what doesn't. That's when you have to take ownership and accountability of it all. Yes, even the shitty things that came to be thanks to your saboteurs. Taking ownership means you can change your situation. And that's a damn powerful thought right there.

Chapter Summary

In this chapter, we explored the eight most common self-sabotage types that origin from your childhood, most likely at any point before the age of seven, as that is the "priming" period in life. Saboteurs want to keep you safe but are not good at it because their strategies are counter-intuitive to what would actually propel you forward. They dislike change and want to keep you in your comfort zone. The more you know about your saboteurs, the better you can overcome them, which we will look at in the next chapters. You've also learned more about the importance of self-awareness, and the key-role it plays in personal improvement.

Chapter 3: A Note of Compassion

Forgiveness doesn't mean you have to agree with hurt and let those who hurt you back into your life. It just means to set yourself free and to move on with grace.

At this point in the book, I want to express the importance of self-compassion. As mentioned in the previous chapter, we may sometimes drift into a negativity spiral and bounce from one self-sabotaging behaviour to the next, finding it harder and harder to break free from our patterns.

Instead of beating yourself up and becoming one of the bullies in "Mean Girls", here is a four-step process that will help you to practise instant self-compassion whenever you catch yourself in self-destruction mode. Later in this book, we will dive into further detail into how exactly we can overcome the saboteurs. But, this process is so crucial that it deserves its own chapter. See it as a little introduction and first-aid kit that you can use for whenever you find yourself in self-sabotage mode.

Practising self-compassion and following this process will support you in developing more self-love, happiness and fulfilment in life overtime.

It has taken me years to really nail down the exact process, but ever since I began implementing these techniques into my day to day, life just looks a little brighter.

So, let's not beat around the bush any longer. Here are the four steps for greater self-compassion, especially in the moments when you feel like you might not deserve it. The truth is, you always do!

Step 1: Forgive yourself and others

One of the best ways to immediately practise kindness and compassion towards yourself is through forgiveness rather than continuously rubbing salt into your wounds. Did you mess up during a presentation? The saboteur reaction would be to say, "H*ow could you, you don't know anything, they will laugh about you and think you are incapable, better work your ass off now to make up for it.*" Instead, reframe this thought and forgive yourself by saying, "I *messed up, and that's okay. It's actually a great learning opportunity. How can I perform better next time?*"

The reason we often tend to get angry at ourselves is because we now know better and see the mistakes we made. Nevertheless, blaming our past selves for not handling the situation as we would now will only feed grudge and hatred towards ourselves. What you got to realise is this: you didn't know back then. How were you even supposed to know? You did the best you could. Anyone else in your shoes would have done the absolute same thing. Forgiveness will help you accept the past and let go of the fact that you cannot undo it. It doesn't mean you just let yourself (or other people) off the hook all the time, but rather to prevent yourself from being consumed by it and instead take your lessons learned to move on. Same with forgiving others, the purpose here is not to see what they did as right, but to release the meaning and power you this experience over yourself. This is a first step to healing yourself.

The sub-step of this one would be: forgive others. Especially if you might have the Victim-Player or Overthinker as saboteurs and tend to hold onto grudges for too long and they rob your energy and wipe that smile off your face.

Step 2: Acknowledge the elephant in the room

I'm referring to the saboteur. As soon as you notice it, you may greet it with, "*Oh, hi, there you are! Thanks for popping up, but I don't need your advice right now.*"

If it comes in the form of a negative emotion that you are experiencing, (because remember: saboteurs always come with a bucket load of negative emotions as part of their "branding package") simply note the emotion you are experiencing. That may sound like "*Hmm I feel anxious right now, my heart is beating really fast and my palms are sweaty. I wonder where this is rooted.*"

Noticing, acknowledging, and naming our negative emotions contributes to how we experience life overall. One of my clients, let's call her Tina, kept all her negative emotions bottled up and buried them very deep down inside of her. She only wanted to experience the good emotions and she only wanted to be seen as a sunny, high spirit and uplifting person. This wasn't very effective, of course, and she had moments when she, in her words, "*just exploded and turned really mean*" to the ones she loved the most. This happened despite her not wanting to be that mean. As we worked together, we took little steps during the sessions to generate more compassion. Tina also practised outside the session to allow the negative emotions to be expressed when they needed to. And *tadaa*: over a year later she felt not only safe in doing so, but she also felt more understood by others and generally happier. The reason for this, my dear, is that without the negative there isn't any positive. Both are needed for the fullest of the human possible expressions. Or how Tina described it "*I feel like a human again*". Because after all, our emotions are what makes us feel truly alive.

Learn to acknowledge the saboteur and the accompanying emotion. The better you can name exactly what you are feeling and experiencing, the easier it is to release it. Simply naming your emotions often is already 80% of the work. To help you with this, I have included The Wheel of Emotions at the end of this chapter. This is just to provide you with a better understanding that there is more to feel than just sad or happy.

Step 3: Consult your best self

As you cleared the space, the next step is to ask yourself, "*What would the version of me at her best do?*" (You might also call her your higher or future self, aspirational identity, inner feminine wisdom, or next level version of you. They are

A Note Of Compassion

all the same and for the sake of simplicity, we go with your best self). What would she do after you messed up a presentation or were procrastinating or maybe you said something mean to someone else because you were controlled by your saboteur? This is where you tap into discernment instead of judgement. For my fellow non-native English Speakers, or anyone who doesn't understand the difference as they are of quite similar origin, here is a simple comparison of the two words:

Judgement is interchangeable with criticism. It is like a final verdict, and more about criticising and accusing. Judgement is also taking an inferior-superior-attitude, fed by the ego (your own ego or other people's egos), and putting yourself above the other person or yourself.

Discernment, on the other hand, is more about seeing things for what they really are, keen perception, and being able to separate one thing from the other. It is about seeking insight and consciously distinguishing what is appropriate and what not rather than just passing on judgement. A question that can help you to find out whether the current thought or behaviour stems from a place of judgement versus discernment is: "Does this thought/behaviour support me to become my best self? If the answer is, "No," then it came from a place of judgement.

Paired with intuition, you get a chance to realign yourself with this best version of yourself with the next action that you take. This might be analysing what you learned from that situation. It could be setting yourself up for success for the next day to break out of the procrastination habit or to genuinely apologise to the other person. Or in other words, you take the one next best step, or make one next best decision at a time.

This is a habit that I do all the time, and not only when dealing with saboteurs. By consulting your best self, you make decisions based on where you want to be, not where you are right now, and this is what keeps you going and moving closer and closer to this version. More on this later, though.

Step 4: Do it

Now, of course, we are here to not only talk the talk but also walk it. Which means: do the action you just have been consulted by yourself to do. If you need help with it, countdown from five and apply *"The Five-Second Rule"* from Mel Robbins. This rule entails that if you have an instinct to act upon something, you have to do it within five seconds. Otherwise, your brain will dump the idea and revert back to automated habits. You can use it in different ways, not only to start doing something but also to interrupt negative thought patterns and self-doubt. It works wonders! In fact, it helped me tremendously when it came to writing this book and my saboteurs wanted to lure me into short-term-pleasure distractions in the form of reading someone else's book whilst sipping tea and nibbling on a biscuit. My saboteurs wanted me to slip into pleasure and sway me off my long-term vision of becoming a published author. The one best thing to break a cycle and change your life is through action. Without it, it is just a sit-and-wait kind of game, and that is not getting you anywhere.

*So, do the thing, break out, stay kind to yourself and
transform your life, one next best step at a time.*

Exercise: Mood Tracker & Practice

In the resource page of this book, you will find a printable PDF
that you can use to track your mood and get better in touch
with your emotions. You can re-use it every month or create
your own version in your journal if you already use one every
day anyway. The goal is to again practise more self-
awareness and notice what is going on on different days, but
don't confuse it with "I need to have happy colours only." Nope.
That's not the purpose of this exercise. It's great if overtime,
your base-level of happiness increases, absolutely. But, at this
point we are only practising more awareness.

Figure: Wheel of Emotions by Geoffrey Roberts

The Wheel of Emotions is a super helpful resource that you can refer back to. You might even want to the tracker with the wheel combined and ask yourself when you feel happy, what kind of "happy" do you feel? When you feel down, what kind of "down"? Practise this for at least a month, or longer if you want to. I still do this short check-in every day, even though I no longer colour any boxes. One of my clients even developed her own incredible version of checking in with her emotions to help her increase her awareness and release them. In her feel-the-feels practice, she checks in with herself and her emotions every hour for thirty seconds. In this short moment, she allows her emotions to bubble up to the surface, and, in her own words, this experience has been "profound". Give it a try and don't shy away from finding your own best method to get more in touch with your emotions. You will find that over time, it will completely shift your experience of life.

A Note On Emotions:

Emotions in themselves are only a co-creation of what's happening within our body and what the brain decides to make sense of based on previous events and experiences. While they are happening within you, they are not you, nor do they show you the full picture of your reality and what's true. Consequently, they should only be seen as messengers to provide insight about what's going on based on the things you do or not do. And whilst you cannot always choose them, you can focus on what is still within your control, then change how you feel about it. Therefore, when it comes to navigating negativity, *you* choose how much power you give your thoughts and emotions.

A great way to look at this is by imagining that your mind is a garden. Right now, you might have some weeds, representing negativity, and flowers, representing positivity, that are growing. You can't control whether weeds pop up, but you can control how you handle them. Remember what you focus on will expand, so if you give the weeds more spotlight than the flowers, they will grow and multiply whilst your flowers might dry up due to neglect. So if you want a flourishing "mind garden" try out the process in this chapter: notice, acknowledge, and uproot the self-sabotaging weeds so that you have free space to choose what you want to feel instead.

Chapter Summary

In this chapter, we acknowledged the importance of self-compassion, self-love, and being kind to ourselves whilst on this journey. As you grow, you will come across new challenges and you will experience new things that you have never experienced before, or that have been bottled up so tightly that it can be tough to look at them again. In order to keep going and reap the benefits along this personal growth journey, kindness and forgiveness will be two of your biggest supporters. You also have a better understanding of your emotions and the messenger-role they play.

Section Summary

- In order to turn your life around, you have to hold up the mirror and do a life audit. Questions like, "How happy are you in this area of life really?" can be a great indicator to see in which areas of your life you are meant for more.

- After you have identified the gap between where you are now and where you want to be, it is time to look at what exactly has been holding you back for so long. Most often, it is due to one's own self-sabotage types that have been initially created in childhood to keep you safe.

- There are eight main self-sabotage types that present themselves in the form of limiting beliefs and thought patterns. The more aware you are of how they show up for you, the easier it will be to overcome them and retrain your brain with new ways of thinking.

- Practising compassion towards yourself will help you make this process of shifting your mindset a lot easier. This includes forgiving yourself, acknowledging what's going on, consulting your best self, and then taking action based on where you want to be.

Section 2:
The Release

Chapter 4: Stop the Self-Rejecting

Your mind is your only limit, so make it limitless.

In the last three chapters, you learned about your self-sabotage types and how to uncover which ones hold you back the most in life. You also started linking them back to childhood memories and learned to look out for them in everyday-life. In this section, and more specifically this chapter, you will learn how to take control over your life back from your saboteurs.

This will require some work on your end in the form of carving out time to do so. But, don't worry: I will guide you through the easiest route to do this with simple steps and prompts.

At this point, I would highly recommend taking out the worksheet you completed about your self-sabotage types, as well as opening up a new page in your journal, or a separate sheet of paper. You have already done 80% of the work by really getting clear on how the saboteur shows up for you and what it says to you. It might say similar things as I described in the list in chapter 2, or something else. There are two sides to breaking out of these thought patterns and wanting to shift your mindset. The first one is all about uprooting the saboteur and the limiting beliefs. This takes a little more time to do, but is highly effective. You have already learned the quick-fix method that you can use in moments when the saboteur pops up. However, the process we are diving into here will lead to more lasting results to not only uproot the limiting belief but also heal. The second side of the coin is breaking the pattern as you notice it, which we will explore in the next chapter more closely.

Part 1: Recognise the Root Cause

Going back to the root cause of a saboteur might not be an easy task for you. It certainly was not easy for me, as I simply cannot remember much from my childhood. My younger years are practically inaccessible to me. I later learned that this is a strategy of the brain to protect itself from pain and stress caused by childhood trauma. However, over time, and with continuous practice, I remembered more and more key memories that contributed to the formation of the several saboteurs that I have.

!!! Before I give you an example from my own experience, I want to put out a word of caution: my example could trigger you too much as it contains mention of self-harm and suicide. If it does, please skip the example altogether. I will let you know in a new paragraph again when it is safe for you to dive back in.

My top saboteur is the critic. I am extremely judgemental towards myself, luckily less so towards others (my value for fairness, equality and accepting others as they was simply always way stronger, but I could not provide the same strength when it came to me). This saboteur was born through several key memories, like being told out of the blue that I was never wanted whilst sitting in the car, or when my dad would compare me to my mum in the same sentence as he was calling her names (sometimes even the whole family just because of the surname), being called dumb and stupid for expressing my thoughts, or less traumatic moments like being told off for wearing what I wanted to wear. But all of this fed into the critic, like fertiliser. It taught me that in order to be worthy (if I ever could be), I had to do more and better. I had to be different and not like anyone else. At the same time, it taught me not to speak up and not use my voice because I wouldn't add value, anyway. It taught me to punish myself for not being good enough. I slipped into self-harming behaviours of which I still carry the scars on my left arm and even suicidal thoughts crept into my mind. I saw no point of me being here if everything was never good enough and pointless anyway. Luckily the one attempt failed and I now know it was because despite it all, I still wanted to live. I still wanted to be happy and live a life worth living, not in the eyes of others, but my own. To do so however, I had to learn to overcome my saboteur as whenever this it popped up, I instantly feel like a piece of shit. Now imagine trying to do life from a place like this. Not very rosy looking, is it? And if you're wondering how the heck you can overcome something like this, I will show you right now.

(To those who skipped the example, you can come back again!)

Part 2: Keep on Giving the Gift of Forgiveness

As we have already touched on in the last chapter, forgiveness is a key part in this whole process when it comes to working with your shadows. So I can only re-emphasise its importance here: Give yourself the gift of forgiveness, but also to others. A practice that has helped me is this: Write a list with everything that has hurt you in the past, whether it was someone else hurting you, or inducing harm on yourself because you think you made a mistake. And after each memory or story-piece, write down:

"I'm sorry, forgive me, thank you, I love you".

This is actually a powerful Hawaiian healing technique called Ho'oponopono. Through this practice, you activate self-love, as well as practice compassion and forgiveness. The word itself means something along the lines of "to correct" or "to put it right". It is a powerful practice that allows you to take back control over your life and free yourself from the painful heavy shackles that keep you stuck. You may even try using it as a mantra every time your saboteur pops up.

In addition, I would love to invite you on a journey into your past through a guided visualisation meditation. In this meditation, you will revisit a key moment in your life that has impacted you the most or is ready to be healed right now. Of course, you can do this meditation several times and visit various places that you want to heal. You will find it on the resource page for this book and you can download it to your phone so you can listen to it offline as well.

If you prefer to do your own meditation, or use certain elements as prompts for your own journey, I included the script below.

Part 3: Visualisation Meditation Script: A Journey Into the Past

To do this meditation, first find a comfortable, seated position with your back straight and feet flat on the ground. Once you are settled into your position, gently let your gaze drop, take a deep breath in, hold at the top for a count to four, and then breathe out through your mouth for six. Repeat this breathing two more times, and let your body relax more and more every time.

As you come back to a normal, breathing pattern, gently close your eyes and relax a little more into your body. Allow your mind and body to be calm and grounded and let go of any leftover tension in your arms, shoulders, neck, jaw, but also your tummy, legs and feet. Let your body settle and relax more and more with every breath you take.

Now that you are in a deeply relaxed state, visualise in your minds eye a light starting to shine from the centre of your chest. Slowly but steady it expands through your whole body, until you are fully filled up with this white and soothing light.

Now imagine a bright beam of this light shining right in front of you. As you follow the direction of the shimmering white and golden beam, you see a path in front of you leading to an elevator. As you step closer and closer to the elevator, you feel more and more relaxed. You feel safe and guided.

Your eyelids feel heavier and heavier as you approach the wide-open elevator doors. You step inside and the doors gently close behind you. You can see different numbers on the control board of the elevator. They all represent your age over the years. Slowly, the elevator is gliding downwards, deeper and deeper into your memories and back into the past. Whilst you are travelling you feel even more relaxed and safe.

You know the elevator will stop at the exact right moment and age that you are supposed to remember right now. You also know you are completely safe and protected by the white light. Gently, the elevator comes to a halt and the doors slide open. You look at the number you stopped at. What age are you at right now?

Then the golden-white beam of light once again is showing you the way, and you step outside the elevator. Right at the same time, the light shines brighter and brighter and paints a picture of a memory when you were that age. You watch as the whole scenery opens once again in front of you. Maybe you are in a room, or outside. As you explore the room, you can see your younger self standing not too far away from you. You watch this memory as if it were a movie playing right in front of you. As you watch your younger self, the light that has been guiding you starts to shine within your younger version, too. As the two beams connect you turn to look at one another. You take a step towards your younger self and embrace it in a big, loving hug. And you say to it, "I'm sorry, forgive me, thank you, I love you". As you say these words, all the pain and heavy emotions that you might have been feeling in this moment slowly disappear. Like bubbles, they gently leave your body and then dissolve in the bright white-golden light around the both of you. Take this moment to tell your younger self anything else that it needs to know right now.

As your younger self listens to you, it starts smiling and says to you as well, "I'm sorry, forgive me, thank you, I love you". As it speaks these words, the light around you starts pulsating and the memory slowly fades away again. You turn around to return to the elevator, ready to step back into your life today, but feeling just a little bit lighter, and more at ease than before. You know that you have begun to heal what needed to be healed right now, and that your life from now on, will be different

The elevator slowly starts to move upwards, and with every breath you take, you feel more and more aligned to this new version of yourself. This version is free of the shackles of the past. This version has only love and compassion for her past. This version is now the author of her own story without being restricted by past unresolved memories. As the elevator comes to a halt once again, you step out and find yourself back in your room and your body. Slowly the light around you is retracting into your body and fills you up to the brim with loving kindness. You can't help but smile. You smile because you know that life will be different from now on. And you keep smiling as you wiggle your toes and fingers, maybe gently stretch and when you are ready, you open your eyes again.

Part 4: Expose and release the lies and start to rewrite your story

Now that you have freed yourself, or at least eased out of some of the chains of the past, the next step is to rewrite your story. All of these memories and beliefs are just that, and nothing more. They don't say anything about who you truly are, and they don't define your worth. In fact, your worth has always been, and always will be, exactly the same. Think of it this way: if you crunch up a £20 note, does it lose its value? No. If you step on it or maybe even rip it, does it lose its value? No. You can go to the bank and exchange it for a new one. Similarly, your initial worth is indestructible for as long as you are here. It's a given. It never changes. To help you see that, we will start re-framing your old thoughts and beliefs, so you change and become the hero of your story again. I once wrote this in a blog post:

"The moment I started to write my own story, based on how I truly see myself and know why I am here, my story started to change." And your moment, my love, is now.

Take out your list with your limiting beliefs again and for each one of them, start by asking yourself: "*Is this really true?*" Psst, the answer is "No". Is it true you are not good enough? Hell no. Is it true you need to work yourself to the ground to be worthy? Nope! Is it true that you are the reason everyone else is fighting? Na-ah, that's on them, my love. Is it true that they will hate you if you say no? No, they most likely aren't bothered by it at all. Is it true you don't deserve to be happy? Absolutely not.

As you can see, these limiting beliefs are basically just a whole bunch of bad lies and far from the truth. To help you see this, and take the first step of actual shifting, write down, "*This is not true, this is a lie.*" Then replace the limiting belief with what you decide to be true from now on. Hereby, you start replacing the limiting thought with a new one, one by one. You can also write down proofs and facts as to why it is true or not.

Below, I rewrote the list from chapter two to give you some inspiration.

- *"I am good enough."*

- *"Who do I think I am, not to do/be this!?"*

- *"Boundaries support me and strengthen my relationships."*

- *"It doesn't matter what others think of me."*

- *"I deserve this."*

- *"My worth is not dependent on how hard I work."*

- *"I am valuable."*

- *"Looking after myself is necessary and a non-negotiable."*

- *"Why do these things always happen for me?"*

- *"From now on I will always be able to stick to my promises."*

- *"I trust myself."*

- *"It gets to be so easy for me."*

- *"I speak my truth and share my opinion with confidence."*

- *"I mean everything I say, and what I have to say has meaning."*

- *"I'm smart and make good decisions."*

- *"Every day I can take one step."*

- *"My time has come now."*

If you fancy an even deeper release-ritual, you may take the list of limiting beliefs, mark them as not true and then burn the list (of course, somewhere safely). It may add another symbolic level for you that from now on, you are no longer chained to these patterns and that it is time to rise into your next–level version. This way, you are physically left with your new belief system only as a reminder of symbolically entering your new era. I did this practice a couple times and *wow,* does it feel good. It also helps to strengthen the new connection in your brain, as you have a visual effect and new memory that feeds into this period of up-levelling. A client of mine did regular release rituals to get rid of any saboteurs and their energy. She would light a sage stick and cleanse her home and herself from the negativity, then call upon her inner strengths to invite uplifting, positive, and empowering energy into her home and herself instead.

You will also find another template in the resources for this book to help you rewrite the limiting beliefs into empowering ones instead. You can download it or just simply take inspiration from its layout to do your thing in the way that is most effective for you.

The key to make this work is to stay open and willing to shift your perception and be available to recognise the patterns, reprogram the paradigms and enter a new experience of life. Allow yourself to keep these doors of possibilities open, and you will be able to enter them into a new reality.

Another powerful exercise is to watch the way you speak and the vocabulary you use. If you find that you often start sentences like this: "*I will never…*" or "*It's so hard to…*", then don't be surprised by your struggles. Instead, switch up the way you speak and allow your words to be more positive and inviting for possibilities to enter. Thus, you train your subconscious to change its language as well.

Chapter Summary

In this very hands-on and practical chapter, you explored the root cause of your limiting beliefs and started to release them through confronting them heads on as lies and instead replacing them with your new truth. This is not an easy task, and it might take you several attempts to finally uproot them. But every time you go debunk your limiting beliefs, it will get ever so slightly easier to let go and evolve.

Before we continue rewriting your story, I feel like it is important to dive into how change really works. It might be as helpful on your journey to levelling up as it was for me.

Chapter 5: Rewiring Your Brain

Everyone is shit at walking at first, but did anyone ever give up on trying? Nope.

Change starts from within. This is a core belief of mine that has accompanied me throughout life for as long as I can remember. In order to make external changes work, or to welcome changes that are placed upon us, we have to look within ourselves to integrate it. Right now, your brain is running a well-trained program. Anything new, in whatever shape or form, will require reprogramming your brain. The problem is that your brain doesn't like change, it will resist. Some changes might come easier to you because there is no other choice and you just have to deal with it. Others might be trickier because you have to convince your brain that this is the right way to go.

And that is also exactly what we will uncover in the next chapters, to not only make it easier on us but also a little less scary for your brain. We want the new thoughts and behaviour patterns to be deemed as safe by your brain so you can integrate them into your daily habits that will build your new reality. First things first, we need to look at how this is all happening inside your mind, and what is needed to kickstart the creation of a new habit.

Change comes in many forms and shapes. The bigger changes in life may include a new job, moving houses, moving abroad, a new relationship, having kids, divorce, losing a job, starting a business. It also may include smaller ones, like trying a new workout, swapping toast for oats for breakfast, changing the clothes you wear, going outside more often, making your own coffee instead of buying one each morning, or even holding your head a little higher when you enter a room instead of slouching. What the big and small changes in our lives all have in common is rather simple: it is a shift away from what we know. Now, whether this is big or small in the grand scheme of things doesn't make much of a difference. Which is why it can actually be really hard building a practice of "only" reading 2-5 pages a day.

In addition, our saboteurs are going bonkers as soon as they sense just the smallest of changes. In fact, they despise change so much that they try everything in their power to keep you "safe" in their eyes. This means when it comes to speaking in front of a camera to sell your services or share your expertise, they will lure you with what they perceive as the better choice in the short-term. This could be sitting on the sofa and scrolling through social media because it is more comfortable and there is no risk of being judged by anyone else in case you say something wrong. Or maybe you don't feel as confident today because your hairdresser messed up the haircut. You can see the saboteurs know all the excuses. They don't know how to think long-term, and this is how they are basically always misaligned with your values and what matters most to you, such as your goals of being healthy. They don't care if their excuses aren't getting you any closer and move you further away from living a life aligned with your values. All they care about is keeping you comfy right here and now. Therefore, it takes an extra amount of effort to convince not only yourself but also your saboteurs that: "Hey, showing up on social media is good for my business and will help me to create the financial and time freedom I crave!"

You could see this as a different description of how your brain works. You see, you programmed your brain your entire life to work exactly as it does now. Most of the programming as we have learned actually happened before the age of seven, in your "priming period". Everything else is what you took on as your "computer program" through societal standards, work, friends and whatever else you spend a lot of time with. Which is why there is so much truth about the phrase, "You are a mix of the five people you spend most of your time with." Have you ever noticed that when dating, and starting a new relationship, after a while you start saying the same things as your partner? I certainly did. My boyfriend also took over some behaviour patterns and words from me. We may also steal certain habits or phrases from our friends. A dear friend of mine, for example, would always greet me with "Aloha!", which I subconsciously copied and now use as well. There is no shame in doing this, by the way. Most of the time, this can't even be controlled because it is a natural human behaviour, as you instinctively seek to be part of a group and get along. You might also find that this is true for both good and bad habits. Raise your hand if you neglect your workout practice because your partner likes to sleep in during the mornings and pulls you back into bed for some extra cuddles and therefore, you don't go. These changes happen more on a subconscious level but need conscious correction.

When it comes to your standard running program, as you are running it again and again, your brain, of course, gets incredibly efficient at. You can imagine it like a well-maintained highway in your head. It is super easy to deliver information and commands along this way and requires less mental energy than a new path. It basically is such a smooth ride for your brain that it becomes an automatic behaviour. Now imagine that you want to change that and present your brain with a jungle path and a machete. Your brain is going to ask you at first, "*What the fuck is this?*" But it accepts the challenge (secretly planning to continue using the easy route though)! The thing is, my love: this is how your highway started off at first, too.

Have you ever learned an instrument? I bet £100 that you were shit the very first time you played it. Everyone is. I'm still surprised my mum's ears didn't fall off when I tried out learning the violin. I was horrible. But the more you practise, the better you get. In our jungle metaphor, the further you go into the jungle and hack away a path, the easier you will find your way the next time. Slowly, over time, you will eventually put some stepping stones down, and maybe build a wider road until you have a new highway. In my violin case, I never got to the highway because I gave up way before that. My "Why" for learning it wasn't strong enough. And over the years, and after countless times of trying out different things like kick-boxing, swimming, ice skating, horseback riding, and more, I trained my brain to not stick to what I set out to do. I would easily loose interest, develop shiny-object-syndrome and have a tough time doing things for longer than a week.

The great news is that with my increasing fascination with all things mindset, psychology, and human behaviour, I managed to retrain my brain to actually stick through the tough times and really go for what I deem worthy of going for and what is truly aligned with my mission. Otherwise, you wouldn't be reading this book right now. Writing a book has been a dream of mine since I was a kid. But it took me twenty-ish years to finally get started and finish it! Another example would be my recent personal record in my weightlifting training. It would not have been possible for if I didn't find a way to build the discipline to create a new "highway" in my brain for these activities to become the new norm.

Let's take a look at how this shift would look in my brain. At first, I built my highway of not sticking to things. My brain was great at dropping new habits and behaviours I wanted to implement. But the magic happened when my "Why" for change was so strong, that I kept on forcing my brain to go into the jungle and hack away at that new path. At the same time as I was venturing into the unknown, my brain neglected to maintain the old route and slowly but steadily "nature took over again" and it turned back into a jungle. Now my brain is primed to be determined as fuck when it comes to achieving and completing something that truly matters to me and where I just know this the right thing for me to do. It also got addicted to seek change and uncertainty because it learned to fall in love with the resulting growth, no matter how scary it is at first. Yes, of course I still hear my saboteurs shouting and fighting, but in the end, I know how to overcome them more and more easily (another example of building a new pathway in your brain). It's the exact same processes you are learning in this book!

Another way to look at this process is through the stages of mastery. They are normally used to describe the process of learning an action, like playing an instrument or building new habits in general. But it works the exact same way for our ways of thinking too, because our thoughts are habitual as well. Experts estimate that we think twelve thousand to ninety thousand thoughts a day, and that a whopping 95% (!!!) of them are the same thoughts as yesterday. Again, this is due to the brain adoring repetition and routine. And as you start shifting you move through these stages of mastery, as explained below.

The Stages of Mastery

The first stage is called "Unconscious Incompetence." Accordingly, right now you don't know what you cannot do, or for our purposes you don't know what you are doing that is harming you. You already completed this stage with learning more about your saboteurs and creating the needed awareness for you to know, "*Hey, I want to change this*".

That's when we get to stage two: "Conscious Incompetence". You now know how you are self-sabotaging, but you still need to learn how to shift your thinking, which is what you are learning in this section. You may also find yourself frustrated at first by how often your saboteurs take over and how tricky it is to redirect your focus (this is the stage where you are hacking your way through the jungle).

The more you practise, however, the closer you get to stage three: "Conscious Competence". You are now aware of your self-sabotaging behaviours; you know the tools to deal with them and you consciously shift from the former to the latter. You also consciously choose a different outcome for yourself, and you know you are getting really good at it.

That's when you then move into stage four: "Unconscious Competence". You shift in your sleep; you are not even worried any more that your saboteurs are holding you back. Their voices become so quiet that you cannot hear them and you walk the path of complete self-trust. You are now fully in control over your perception of life. Thoughts like, "You are not good enough," don't pop up that often any more, or if they do, you know immediately that it's not true and you let them pass.

So, you see: because you trained your brain to be what it is right now, you can train it to be completely different in a year's time. You now have the awareness of your saboteurs, limiting beliefs, and any thought patterns that are not of any service to you. You also explored the root cause of your saboteurs to truly uproot the weeds in your mind, and you understand that it takes consistent practice and tending after your mind to grow and strengthen the new patterns.

Luckily, this consistent practice doesn't have to be super difficult or tricky to do. In fact, you already tried out one way of "shifting" in chapter one. Remember the breathing exercise? Here are three more very similar exercises that you can do to effectively break out of a current "thought-slump" when being hijacked by your saboteurs. Each time you do these kinds of exercises, you break the cycle and strengthen your new connection in your brain. Whilst it first needs conscious effort, the more you do it, the easier it will be, and eventually it will require less and less conscious effort as your subconscious integrates it.

Exercise 1: Observation

Sit with your back up straight and your feet flat on the floor. Take a deep breath to ground yourself and fixate your gaze onto an object right in front of you. Start to observe it in all its detail, notice its shade of colour and shape by following its outline with your eyes. Be curious about the surface and notice whether it is shiny, matt, rough or smooth. Does it look soft or hard? Reach out and touch the object and feel it. Does it match with your observations? What is its temperature? Does it feel warm or cold? Is it light or heavy? How does it feel on your skin? What else is there to notice about this object that perhaps, you didn't notice before? Don't overthink it, simply observe and tune in with your sense of sight and touch.

Exercise 2: 5-4-3-2-1

This exercise you can also find as recorded audio walking meditation in the resource portal. However, you can do this exercise anywhere and at any time. I have been doing this specific exercise for over six years now and even taught it to others at the company I used to work for. It also serves as a staple in my coaching session when working with clients because it's such an easy way to both get back into your body and reconnect with your senses. It distracts your thought spiral and brings you back into the present moment. You may also find that it will help you appreciate your surroundings and the experience of life just a tiny little bit more. I often used to check-in with my senses during walks along the coast in Espoo, Finland and it never failed to make me appreciate the fresh air and beautiful scenery a little more. Before I drift too far off, here is how you can do this exercise yourself. No matter where you are right now, follow these instructions to give it a try:

1. Focus and list in your mind five things you can see. (For example: this book if you have a physical copy, or the device you are reading on.)

2. List four things you can feel on your body or in form of emotions. (For example: your super cosy jumper that you are wearing, or a calm sensation)

3. Now list three things you can hear. (For example: cars or kids playing outside your house.)

4. Next list two things you can smell. (For example: the "fresh linen" scented candle you just lit.)

5. Lastly, list one thing you can taste. (For example: a sip of your morning coffee.)

Exercise 3: Release

If tapping into your senses might not work as well for you, you can try this exercise that taps further into your subconscious mind. It's a tool used in RTT (Rapid Transformational Therapy), and the beauty of it is that you can use it within one to three minutes without anybody around you noticing. To do this exercise, either close your eyes or keep a soft and steady gaze at a point in front of you. Then, allow the negative energy of your saboteur to come up, or allow yourself to be fully consumed by the negative thoughts and respective feelings for three seconds. As if you were to turn the volume up on the radio very briefly and then turn it back down again. After those three seconds, take a deep breath in for a count of four, hold at the top for another count of four, then think and see the word "release" in your mind's eye as you breathe out with a big sigh. In yoga, this is called a cleansing breath. Repeat this breathing exercise for another two times. Each time before you breathe out, think of the word "release", and at the same time, release your breath and therefore cleanse your body from that energy.

Exercise: Managing the Thought Trains

Another metaphor that might be useful to you would be to imagine every thought is a train and you are at the train station. (For some reason, I always envision the scene in Harry Potter and the Deathly Hallows Part Two (2011) when Harry talks to Dumbledore after he gets attacked by Voldemort. It's such a serene, tranquil place, but yours might look completely different.)

When a thought pops up in your mind, it drives into the station and stops right in front of you. You then have the choice to board it, or to just send it off its way. For example if your saboteur sends you thoughts like, "*You are not good enough, you need to do better or more, work harder*", you get to choose whether you board this train. If you'd like, you can let it go on its way and choose to board the train of your liking that says, "*I am good enough, I am worthy, and I am loveable.*" Again, I cannot say this enough: the more you practise this, the easier it will get. It is totally normal that every now and then, you board the first train. Luckily, you know the steps that allow you to get off again at the next stop, and board the train you actually wanted.

The purpose of these exercises is to disrupt self-sabotage mode. In a way, it's like taking a step back, breathing, and then returning with more clarity.

It provides you with a moment of time to choose which path you want to go down, rather than sprinting full tempo and doing the first best thing your brain suggests.

And you can imagine which one it will suggest if one of the paths is a well-maintained highway compared to a jungle path. But, through slowing down, you take back control over this almost automatic process, and you get to choose. Do you choose to go down the saboteur route? Or will you strengthen your new pathway? Not only can you change course for the actions you are about to take, but also the thoughts that you accept as your truth.

All of these exercises are also various ways to regulate our nervous system. First, you create the awareness about your sensations and emotions that you are experiencing and then you use different mindfulness-tools as described in this chapter to respond to the stressor in a healthier way. Through uprooting and rewiring your brain, you are then starting to undo the previous effects of the trauma and deeply ingrained stress responses. All the while, you are growing more resilient and in turn preventing chronic stress. In other words, you nip the gremlins in the butt through mindful regulation.

Chapter Summary

In this chapter, you learned how to retrain and therefore change your brain. There are two main paths to this, a deep uproot and continuous practice (both always paired with compassion) to break the cycle of self-sabotage. You are now familiar with the stages of mastery and are well-equipped with several exercises to regulate your nervous system and put a halt to the next time your saboteur pops up and changes your course of action, one step after the other. The more you do it, the easier it will be over time. These are tools for life. They are not a one-off fix, but more like an addition to your toolkit to have the best experience of life possible.

Section Summary

- There are four steps to release limiting beliefs, and so far we have explored three of them: Recognise (notice how you are holding yourself back), Release (break free from the shackles of these limiting beliefs through forgiveness and debunking them as lies), and Reframe (rewrite the belief into an empowering one and start replacing it with something that accelerates your growth rather than hinders it).

- Your brain and your saboteurs dislike change, but it is not impossible. In fact, the same way you trained your brain to think as it does now, you train it to think in a new way.

- Any new neural pathway you create is at first, only a very thin thread. The more you use this new pathway, the stronger the thread gets until it becomes second nature.

- Dealing with your saboteurs is simply another description of regulating your nervous system and knowing how to respond to stress with mindfulness practices.

Section 3:
The Breakthrough

Chapter 6: Your "Why" to Change

"Whatever you are not changing, you are choosing"
Laurie Buchanan

In the last chapter, we explored what change looks like in our mind and brain. You also saw me mentioning the "Why", which is a crucial success factor when it comes to creating lasting change. Hence, we will explore this a little further in this chapter, as well as how to set yourself up for success in creating new thought patterns and belief systems that are not controlled by your saboteurs.

I don't know about you, but when someone ever asked me to do something that 1. I didn't want to do, 2. I didn't see any value in doing it for myself nor others and 3. It didn't align with my personal values or was very contradictory to how I wanted to do something, I would either not do it at all, procrastinate until it got forgotten, or heavily challenge the task at hand.

The best example is when my dad had organised an interview for me for a job with a company. Yes, that might have been nice of him, and I did appreciate the effort. But, did I actually schedule a call with that guy? No. Here's why: I didn't want to do it. I didn't see the value in it because it wasn't aligned with what I wanted to pursue as my career back then (it was something with chemistry and working in a lab; I wanted to be in business or finance). I also wanted to do it myself and not have to rely on him. Or in short, there was no power to the "Why" I should do this. And just to provide you with a happy ending to this: I kept on applying for the jobs and roles I truly wanted (back then, not any more) and landed my apprenticeship at my dream company. I got what I wanted, it was aligned with my values and goals, and I did it my way. In other words, my "Why" and therefore, my intrinsic motivation was a lot stronger.

"*How does this relate to changing your mindset and your limiting beliefs?*" I hear you asking. Well, exactly the same. But let's first differentiate intrinsic and extrinsic motivation.

If my dad would have put more pressure on me, or if I threw my own "Why" out of the window in order to make him happy, then that would have been extrinsic motivation. In other words, it is any form of motivation that does not come from within you. Intrinsic motivation, on the other hand, is deeply driven by your personal values and your goals. Most of all, you experience joy in doing it and it therefore contributes to your personal fulfilment in life. James Clear put it this way in his book "*Atomic Habits*": "The highest possible form of intrinsic motivation is when you identify as the person who lives by her values and follows her dreams."

Another example of extrinsic motivation would be if you only want to ace at your job to get a pay rise, and not because you actually enjoy it. Or, it could be that you want to lose weight because you feel pressured by society, not because you actually want to be healthy and feel great in your skin. Or, it could be because someone just told you to do it, even though you don't want to. Of course, there are instances where you just have to bite your tongue and do the action. There is no black and white to this, there are plenty of grey areas. But, when it comes to changing your mindset, up-levelling yourself and acing your game in life, external motivation alone won't cut it. You gotta want it. And you need to want it badly. (Side note: you don't have to want it bad all the time. Sometimes, you only need to strongly desire it enough in the beginning until it becomes the nature of how you do things).

How do you crave something bad enough so you simply don't see another way other than rolling up your sleeves and getting to it?

Well, you get crystal clear on your "Why" you want to do it. And if you now think, "*What the hell, how do I even do this?*", you are not alone. It took me years, (yes, *years*) to finally grasp the concept of it properly. At first, I was doing it subconsciously, not knowing that I would stick to some things because my "Why" was stronger compared to other things. But the beauty of hindsight is that you look back and it all just makes sense as you can pinpoint what has led to what outcomes.

Exercise: Find Your "Why"

To find your "Why", work through at least some of the questions below. Take out your journal again, or a piece of paper, or open a GDoc and scribble down whatever opens up for you. To get the most out of this exercise, think back to the area of your life that you want to change and get closer to a ten.

If you remember, I asked you questions like "*How does it feel to be at this rating in your life right now?*", or "*What would be different if it were a ten, how would you feel?*". These are already great pointers to find out your intrinsic motivation as to why you seek change. The following questions will help you to get even clearer and more specific with it.

Questions to find your "Why":

- *Why do you want to change?*

- *What is the cost of staying where you are right now?*

- *If you don't change anything, what will life continue to look like in one, five, ten or thirty years from now?*

- *Imagine that you are on your deathbed. What would you want to have chosen to do?*

- *What do you want to be remembered for?*

- *What are you willing to take a stance for?*

- *How will life be different if you start doing X now?*

- *What will be possible for you?*

- *Why is this important to you?*

- *Why is now the perfect time to do this or get started?*

- *How can you fall in love with the process?*

- *Who are you evolving into by implementing this change?*

- *What will you be most proud of?*

- *How bad do you want it, really?*

Working through these questions will unlock a motivation within you that is going to feel like a fire. The "hotter" you get it to be from the get-go, the harder it will be for your saboteurs to come out and try to extinguish it. This is what will keep you going, even when it feels super hard. This is what encourages you to sit down and start writing another page (or sentence) in your book, even if you have writer's block and might delete it later. Your "Why" is what fuels your discipline to keep on showing up for your employees, even if times are currently hard or you don't feel like it. Your "Why" for working, training, reading, cooking, writing, career, dancing, being a parent, etc., is highly connected to your best version of yourself, your purpose, and your mission and vision in life. Once you get this part sorted, everything won't magically be easier, but it will feel like this is what you were meant to do all along! In other words, it just feels so right.

For example, my "Why" for this book is that it has been a childhood dream. It is aligned with what I want to have accomplished late in life (being a published author). I *love* writing and it gives me so much joy and fulfilment. It aids my mission to help more women do amazing things in their lives. It fuels my self-belief, it is proof that I can do hard things and if I can do it so can you.

If you want to learn even more about your "Why", I highly recommend reading the book "*Start with Why*" by Simon

Sinek. He also nicely breaks down, in much greater depth, how this will help you with the "How" and "What".

Now that we have your "Why" sorted, the next step is to set an intention and a goal (in fact, you might even set several intentions for one goal).

Exercise: Set Your Goal and Intentions

Goals and intentions are similar, yet also very different from each other. A goal is a specific, performance-based outcome. I often set SMART goals with my clients, or for this very book I set myself AIM SMART goals. Before you moan and mark it as "outdated", give it a go. If done right, this process ensures that the goal is specific, measurable, achievable, relevant, and time bound. The addition of AIM means that you also decide on your "Acceptable" outcome (the minimum outcome you want to achieve), the "Ideal" outcome (best case scenario) and the "Middle" (mix between the acceptable and ideal outcome). All aspects that will help you to achieve it.

Remember your goal that you picked at the beginning? Use this moment to set your AIM SMART goal for your life at a ten in your chosen area.

Example: I will write a book of around 50,000 words or 200 pages by December 2023. This word count goal is split into milestones for each month. 14,000 in October and 32,000 in November. To reach this goal, I set up a daily writing practice from ten to eleven AM and need to reach a minimum of 600 words every day. I am doing this because it has always been my dream to become a published author, and I love writing.

This goal ticks all of the boxes. It is specific, measurable, achievable, relevant, and time-bound. In regards to "time-relevant", I do want to point out that a fixed deadline is only truly achievable for goals that are 100% in your control even if life "happens". The reason being, if too many other external factors are at play, you do need to take into account the possibility and flexibility of not hitting that target.

My "Acceptable" goal: stick to my writing practice even if I don't reach my deadline in December to build the habit of writing.

My "Ideal" goal: stick to my writing practice and/or exceed my daily word goal and finish the book as intended in December, before Christmas. I also regularly update my audience on social media and bring together a group of people as beta readers/editors.

My "Middle" goal: hit my writing goal every day, stick to my practice, and bring together a group of people as beta readers.

That's your goal done. An intention, however, is more about your present internal feeling state, or who you are in the process of working towards your goal. It is like setting the tone or theme on a day-to-day, weekly, monthly or yearly basis. I love setting intentions for any day. Sometimes, I choose an affirmation that speaks to me. Sometimes, it is only one word or I pull an oracle card and make that my intention for the day ahead or a bigger project. In regard to the writing of this book, I did and do all of the above. My overall intention is to feel and identify as an author. Daily intentions included flow, creativity, or trust. The card I pulled was called "Lost Lands" and was a constant reminder for the entire time as I was writing that I should trust my path as author and the wisdom I must share because I have done it before. It definitely is the right amount of "woo-woo" I needed in order to make sure I trusted whatever flew out of my fingers and onto the keyboard.

Questions to help you set an intention:

- *What intention would you like to set for the journey to achieving your goal?*

- *How do you want to be and feel in the process?*

- *What strength within you do you want to call upon?*

Setting goals and working towards them is the key action to take if you want to break out of the daily autopilot and of course, if you are longing to live a life of meaning and purpose. The impact this can have on your day to day is significant.

For my client Holly, it most certainly was. At the beginning of our coaching relationship, Holly didn't know what she wanted. In her words, she wanted *"life to be better"*, but couldn't pin down exactly what that would look like. Whenever I tried to encourage her to dream about her goals and simply imagine what life would be like once it was "better", she was quick to rationalise why she couldn't achieve that or how impossible and hard it would be for her based on past experiences. Which as you now know, is a completely natural thing to happen, as the brain loves reasoning. Whatever is stored as a memory is the easiest program for it to run. So, to slowly rewrite this program, we set smaller milestones that she could see as at leas a possible option for her.

Step by step, she increased her confidence and became more and more certain about several things in her life and how she wanted them to look like. This helped her finally say, "*I know what I want!*". And together, we worked out three goals to achieve during our time together in the areas of personal growth, career, and health. Not only did this provide her with direction in life and more motivation, but recognising her own growth and transformation led her to experience life on a new level. My absolute favourite messages I ever received from her are: "I *wake up with so much joy,*" and "*My life is so fun and exciting!*" This is a big deal, and I couldn't be more proud, because I know that this woman is going places. She now knows how to show up for herself, make herself a priority and she doesn't give up. These are incredible strengths that will make her transformation even more remarkable, and they all come from the choice of not living on autopilot any more, setting goals she has a strong "Why" to achieve, and continuously working towards them.

The Power of #Delulu (Trend Word for "Delusional")

Whilst yes, your goals should be smart and achievable. This doesn't mean that they need to be small. They can be big. Huge, in fact! I would even invite you to think about a goal that just gets you freaking excited and sounds super crazy. I dare you to be delusional for a moment. Take my book, for example. Yes, I wanted to write a book. However, my #delulu goal is to produce a debut book with many more to follow. Heck, I want to travel the world promoting my books! I want to have several. I want to be a bestselling author. These are big goals. They are also attainable goals. They are indefinitely possible. What's simply unattainable would be to say, "I want to write a 100k word-count book within a week from a hammock in Bali." Maybe the hammock part is possible, but the other parts are not. That's where the other elements of the AIM SMART goal will help to put the needed element of sense into it.

Chapter Summary

In this chapter, you got clear on your motivation to change your life around and lit the fire that will keep you going throughout the process of up-levelling yourself and your life. The stronger the "Why", the less likely you will waver and fall back into old habits and settle for less than you deserve. This is the key to change. In addition, having a clear goal provides not only guidance in life, but ultimately leads to more purpose and fulfilment. And there's no better feeling than realising that *hey, you actually can do this!*

Chapter 7: Your Inner Superpowers

You are as capable as you believe you are.

Now that you understand your mission and know why you are embarking on this new journey to reach your goal, it is time to get you fully equipped and unlock your utmost potential. And surprise: these powers are already within you. Yes, you already have all that you need. And I will show you how to call upon your strengths, and even turn your weaknesses into one of your strongest allies on your path.

Have you ever wondered why it is that you feel drawn to certain people and admire specific traits that they have, longing to have the same or at least a fraction of it yourself? The truth is, my dear, you already do have this. You are drawn to these people because subconsciously, you see yourself in them. Furthermore, you attract what you are. Therefore, if you see people popping up around you in your life, then most likely, it is because you are upgrading into this new version of yourself right now. And if you just thought, *"That's not true, I can never be like Caroline; she is way more confident than I am,"* then that's the exact reason why you cannot presently see this strength within yourself. You're in saboteur-mode. If you were to look at it from your best self however, you can see that actually you do have these qualities if you embrace them. Of course, I'm not talking about skills like skiing or painting. Those are however learnable and can be improved through practice. But confidence, self-belief, trust, honesty, or love are qualities we all are born with. They are an integral part of your best self. To start unlocking them, ask yourself what would your best self say? Would she doubt her abilities too? Or would she say, "*Heck Yeah, I'm a confident, sassy ass person!*" I shall vote for the latter.

Your best self knows and believes that she can do tough things. She would never downplay your abilities and will always encourage you to continue growing. The word "never" does not exist in her vocabulary. Instead, she says "*try*" or adds the small but powerful word "yet" – "*I'm not that confident, yet!*"

She might have some words of discernment for you, but she would never judge you. That's what your saboteurs do. They say, "*You are not good enough.*" Your best self says, "*Try anyway; you will learn along the way.*"

Remember, the saboteurs want to keep you small, yet your best self wants to see you grow infinitely. And the cool thing is, every single human being has a best self from the moment they are born. She cannot be taken away. She cannot be silenced, and she will never leave your side. Why? Because you already are that version of you. She has always been there. But as you grew up, you started putting layers around her, like an onion. Layers of social standards, external expectations, traumas maybe and other experiences that contributed to you playing smaller than you actually are. It's time to shed those layers again.

I'm sure you have noticed the moment when she peeked out between those layers. The moments when you felt like you were completely in flow, everything was just going perfectly well, you were aligned, and felt the serotonin rushing through your veins. This is your best self trying to show you what you are capable of doing, being, and experiencing.

The funny thing is that as you evolve into your next best version of yourself, you actually are simply getting closer to who you have always been.

That version of you is not a new person or hugely different from you. It is you at your most authentic and true core. Pretty cool, right? You might have experienced her peeking through even more as you were working through previous exercises. The more layers you peel away, the easier it will be for her to spread her energy and fill your entire being. We are in the midst of the process to tear the walls down from the outside, so the reasonable next step is to give her more power again from the inside. Which is exactly what we are tackling in this chapter.

I hope that these last words have already stirred something up within you. A feeling of possibility, another spark of energy and motivation, another drop of fuel in your fire, another proof of how incredibly capable you are, my love. This is you building and strengthening your self-trust and self-belief. This is you starting to realise your potential to turn the keys to unlock the doors. This is you becoming your best self.

(Side note: I'm getting goosebumps as I'm writing this because I am so damn excited for you to step into your power. My eyes are getting watery because I can already see your light shining like crazy, I'm already so proud and in awe of you. You are amazing, my dear!)

Now it is time to put this energy to good use in a few different exercises to activate your inner strengths, and most importantly, your true inner essence.

For this purpose, I have prepared another visualisation meditation for you, which you can find on the resource page for this book. However, I also wrote down a similar process here that will allow you to activate your best self without doing a visualisation. If you fancy, you can even try both ways, but make sure to not skip it. It is too important to be ignored. If any of your saboteurs are crying out loud right now because they are scared to have to give up their power, then great. Let them. It's not their time any more, they have done their deed. Now it's time for you to claim back your utmost potential.

Exercise: Activate Your Best Self

Take out a piece of paper and draw a circle on it. This circle represents your life. Now, draw another circle in the middle of that one, this circle represents the CEO running your life. Now answer these questions:

- *How do you want this CEO to run your life?*
- *What leadership qualities do you need/want/admire the most?*

- *If you think of other people who are leaders, what are the key characteristics that you admire in them?*

- *How does this CEO show up?*

- *How do you want it to support you in your life?*

- *How does it navigate challenges?*

Write down everything that comes up for you, don't overthink it or question whether you have this quality right now or not. Once you write down all of the qualities, feel free to sort them or cross out doubles so that you are left with a list of pure empowerment and a representation of what true leadership looks like for you. Then stand up, and imagine you are now embodying all of these qualities. Stand as this leader, move as this leader, and speak as this leader. Fully notice how it feels to stand in your power right now.

Again, saboteurs have a broadcast break right now. This moment is all about you and your best version of yourself. To take it to another level, find a metaphor or a picture that would best describe your best self. Print it out or draw it and connect it with the qualities that you wrote down so that you can always tap back into it.

This is a pretty powerful exercise, isn't it? I want to share an example from one of my clients that clearly showcases how things have changed with the activation of her best self.

When Catherine joined the Zoom call, she was ridden by her saboteurs. I could immediately tell that there was a heavy weight on her shoulders. She was slumping and slouching and the resonance levels were sub-zero. She didn't move around much, and as she was speaking about her topic on showing up as an authentic leader, she grew even smaller. That's the visual effect that saboteurs have on you. I let her speak for a while, to allow the emotions to be expressed and to allow the saboteurs to have their stage light. As soon as the saboteurs made their point, I invited her to shake them off and ban them from the room. We completed a short meditation to disrupt the current thought process and got her back into a neutral state. She wasn't as small any more and found her equilibrium again.

Next, we worked through the visualisation exercise and called upon her best self. The more specific we got in her abilities and qualities, the more Catherine stood her ground. As she felt the energy of her true inner essence and stepped into flow, the more a smile started to appear on her face. After we finished her exercises, her posture and demeanour had completely changed. She now stood proud, activated, aligned and was oozing with energy. She was beaming through my screen from another country and her energy made my skin prickle and my eyes tear up. We both shed some happy tears, baffled about what just happened. Catherine had, for the first time ever, experienced herself in utmost alignment with her best self and activated her full inner feminine wisdom. There were no signs of saboteurs or any limiting beliefs at this moment. It was just her at her best. To never forget this moment, I invited her to find an object she could use as a reminder of how she felt in that current moment. She found a small, plastic flower that she has kept to this day as her reminder of her best self. She uses it to call upon her strengths whenever needed.

Your best self is the symbol of two main characteristics. I call them Self-Leadership and Self-Love. The first means exactly what it says. You are leading yourself. You are leading by example, standing up for what matters most to you, following your purpose, and taking full responsibility over your experience on this planet. You are the CEO of your own life. You run the show, and you play your own game. (Side note: we are never playing any other game. There is only one, and that is yours. You are stepping into self-leadership and therefore give zero fucks about other people's or society's games!)

Self-Love is an appreciation of one's own worth or virtue and proper regard for and attention to one's own happiness or well-being. Self-love is about appreciating and accepting who you are, as you are. This includes your history, your dreams, your mistakes, your values, your strengths, your flaws, your accomplishments, your freckles, your hair, your little toes, your body shape, your voice, your style, your choices, your taste of music, your favourite food, your least favourite food, and anything that makes you, *you.* The more often you detach your worth from anything external, and instead focus on intrinsic validation about what you believe and know is true about you, the more you set yourself free.

Fostering self-love is one of the core lessons that each and every one of us must learn. It is the foundation for more love to come, stay, and go. The more profound we get it to be, the less anything else can disturb not only our love for who we are but also what we do. It is standing up for yourself, setting boundaries, taking care of the mind, soul, body, and spirit. It's about being yourself unapologetically, knowing yourself better than anyone else, treating yourself as your most important human in life, learning from mistakes, and following your dreams and passion.

The truth is, the most important relationship you will ever have is the one with yourself. You have it from the moment you are born until you take your last breath. And the other reason why this is so important is that we can only love others up to the level we love ourselves. We can only allow love into our lives up to the level we love ourselves.

In choosing your symbol or persona for your best self, you are choosing the best representation of the attributes self-leadership and self-love. It is an expression of who you are at your core and at your best. As we are on the journey of "peeling the onion", it is also who you are "re-becoming". This is the process of bridging the "gap" between your current and best self. But, as I indicated before, there are more resources that you can access at any moment.

Your Allies

Let's give your best self some extra support and call upon any other more specific strengths and inner resources that you want to be of aid to you on this quest to reach your goal. These come in the form of allies, or how I like to call them: your very personal team of superheroes.

My team of superheroes consists of different personas or even objects. There is no limit to your creativity in who you want on your team. It depends on what resonates most with you. Hence, in my team, you will find my best self, which is a Lara Croft wizard version with long, grey hair, a cloak, and a hat. For me, she symbolises being at the right place at the right time and doing the exact right thing that is needed in the moment. She also represents doing life on her terms, breaking the norm, being open-minded and craves to use her powers for the greater good. Or, to put it differently: she represents ultimate alignment with my values and my authentic self and reminds me to always follow and trust my intuition and believe in myself. Other allies include a superhero from an anime that uses fire as his power, and he is my representative for my masculine energy. I have a feather that oozes softness, kindness, ease, and flow. Lastly, my inner child that stands for playfulness and joy.

As you can see, your very own team of superheroes, a.k.a. inner strengths can consist of anything. You can be super creative or very pragmatic. My clients, for instance, have confidence needles (for as you might have already guessed: extra confidence), little Buddhas (for Zen and calm) or even dragons (for inner power). Next to activating your best self, this is one of my favourite exercises, because it is super fun and easy, yet extremely impactful. Are you ready to meet your superhero team?

Exercise: Activating Your Inner Strengths

There are two (or actually 3) ways to find your allies, and we will explore them all to hopefully find most of them. However, you may find that as you continue to work on your goals that you need to create another ally, or that some of them are actually one and the same.

The first and easiest route to find your allies is by asking yourself what are your weaknesses?

For example, you find you are not confident enough. Awesome, "confidence" is ally numero uno. Or, you find that you can't relax and have a constant need to stay busy and do something. Great, "Relaxation" is your ally numero dos. Or, you find you are too bubbly, always oversharing and talking too much. Excellent, "Coolness" is your ally numero tres.

The key with this exercise is to first note down the key-strength you feel like you are missing, just so that we have a starting point. We will evolve these further after we explore the second way of finding your allies.

For this one, think about the strengths that brought you to where you are now, or what has helped you get through to the other side during tough times. These things may just make you extremely happy and put you into a better mood and shift your energy to a higher vibration.

Here are some examples:

- Even though being made redundant was hard, you kept a positive attitude and appreciated the support you received from friends and family. There are two allies in this: "positivity" and "appreciation".

- You have a great knack to talk to people and a wonderful network, this has helped you to form incredible friendships and find your dream job. This ally could be "connection".

- You absolutely adore singing, dancing, listening to music or even playing an instrument. It just makes you super happy and you enjoy every second of it. "Music" might be the ally in disguise here.

As mentioned, there are three ways to find your allies. You've already explored the question that can uncover more allies of yours, which is: "*What matters most to you?*" Yes, I am talking about your values. In my case, this would be freedom, impact, and authenticity. Pull up your notes on this question and circle any values that can become a part of your inner superhero team.

After you have worked through these exercises, make a list. In our case, we collected the following potential allies:

- *Confidence*

- *Relaxation*

- *Coolness*

- *Positivity*

- *Appreciation*

- *Connecting*

- *Music*

- *Freedom*

- *Impact*

- *Authenticity*

In the next steps, look at each of these words and work through the following three questions. These questions will help you get crystal clear on how each ally appears in your life. This may help you decide whether you want it in your team, or not.

- *How does this value support you on your journey?*

- *What does this ally look like?*

- *What does it feel like, if you are in the energy of this ally?*

- *What empowering statement or motto does this ally have?*

And that's it! You did it! Your team of superheroes is finally complete. Now, it's time to explore how you can use and activate them whenever you need them the most. Your best self and your allies can also be simply seen as different energies you can activate. Emotions are in fact vibrations, and vibrations are the rippling effect of energy. By now, you should be familiar with the energies of the saboteurs and how different they feel compared to your best self. As a reminder, saboteurs feel heavy, and they are connected to mostly negative emotions like frustration, anger, sadness, guilt, and shame.

On the other hand, your best self and your allies represent confidence, bliss, happiness, joy, lightness, ease, and flow.

Hence, when it comes to channelling one of your superheroes, all you need to do is to get into a state of their energy. The key here is to feel and embody the energy of your superheroes.

Exercise: Mini-Visualisation to Power Up

This is another mini-visualisation exercise that you will find an audio version of on the resource page. I invite you to learn how to do this practice on your own as well. Just in case you want to channel your inner strengths right in the middle of a meeting to channel courage to speak up and share your opinion, are about to jump on a sales call with a new potential client and want to state your increased prices with full confidence, or when you are close to getting into an argument with your partner and want to navigate the situation with love and compassion.

Before we call upon an ally or your best self, let's get back into a neutral space. To do so, gently close your eyes, if you feel comfortable. Take a couple of deep breaths to slow down your heartbeat and relax. Then, focus all of your attention on your toes. Connect with each and every little toe of yours. Shift your focus like a magnifying glass across your shins, knees, thighs and up to your hips until you reach your chest area. Go down your arms, then focus on each of your fingers as well before you move back up. You will finish this body scan at the top of your head.

Now that you are grounded and calm, think of the challenge or situation you are facing and ask yourself which of your allies would be of best service to you right now. You might even envision them all sitting at a round table. Take your time to check in with each of them and find the right fit. Once you make your choice, envision yourself stepping up to your ally and touching it. As soon as you stretch out your hand, a bright white light will engulf you and slowly absorb into your body. You can feel the energy of this ally grow within you. It's like your body has been activated and is flooded with this incredible energy. You feel capable, you feel strong, and you feel confident. You are ready to tackle this challenge with your allies' help.

Exercise: The Round-table

If you are more of a visual or logical person, you can try the following. On a piece of paper, write down your challenge in one or two sentences and circle it. Around this circle, write down all of your allies' names including your best self. Check in with each of them to find out which one has the best advice for you right now. As you choose one of them by circling it in another colour, imagine in your mind's eye that you are being flooded with its energy through the paper. Take three deep breaths, and with each breath, you will feel this energy flood your entire body. You will see an example of this below, but there is also a downloadable template of this exercise available on the resource page, too.

Your Inner Superpowers

Template: Round-table Exercise

However, I encourage you to make this sheet on your own. Create your personal ritual to activate your allies, as long as you feel that switch in your energy. You will also notice that the more you practise this shift, the easier it will get. After a while, you may only need to think briefly about the ally you want to call upon to activate its strengths within you.

One of my clients even purchased a ring as a way to always remind herself of the values she wants to embody more of as well as the energies she wants to tap into as a leader. This ring represents her new era in which she decided she will be more patient and composed, like a queen. Whenever she finds herself in old patterns of feeling impatient or too candid with her private life in a professional environment, this ring immediately reminds her how to deal with things as her best version of herself. If you are into tattoos like me, you can get a small tattoo somewhere slightly more visible, like on your wrist or arm, to always remind yourself of who you are choosing to become at any point in time.

Now that you know how to channel your best self and allies, I want to provide you with three additional energies that are already a part of your team of superheroes.

The Feminine, Masculine and the Inner Child

One thing I wished someone had taught me earlier on this journey was how the heck to work my feminine and masculine energy, as well as how to look after my inner child's energy. Because being aware of how to best use them is a game-changer.

First up, here are some brief explanations about these energies, so you know exactly what I mean by them. Nowadays, I feel like most people already know or are actually in full swing of their masculine energy. Being productive and determined, having structure and plans, powerfully pushing limits and working hard. We live in a fast, ever-changing world and the stigma we are taught is to work harder than anyone else to stay afloat. We are taught to be better, faster, and stronger than anyone else to make it. It's all about doing. The more you do, the better. To me personally, the best visual of masculine energy is fire. And the best motto to put it into one sentence would be: "Get shit done".

On the other side we have the feminine energy. This energy represents being. It's about receivership, joy, flow, rest, nourishment, love, ease, creativity, and intuition. To me, this is represented by water, and the motto is "Go with the Flow". Which, as you know, I had to re-learn to tap into, to access and allow into my life again.

This same scenario goes for many of my clients. We have been scrutinised for years and years when we expressed our femininity. In order to make it in a world run by mainly men, we had to adopt the same characteristics, hiding "unfavourable" personal traits. No wonder we are now struggling to embrace it. No wonder we are burning out. No wonder we feel fake, because all we do is try to force our way of being into a single form of energy. But, that simply doesn't work. This goes for both women, and men. There is not just one way of doing things. Finding the sweet spot in these energy balances is what unlocks your full potential and genius.

The third one in this bundle is the inner child's energy. This one we are all born with. As we grow up and learn to navigate this world, it trickles away. This energy is all about curiosity, learning, connecting, playing, and being free of judgement. Embracing the inner child energy is to be full of wonders and dreams. My personal picture of this energy is a rainbow, and its motto is "Life is Magical".

During the first session, I often ask my clients, "*What are your dreams?*" and invite them to give themselves permission for a moment to dream again as if they were a child. Try it yourself. Think back to when everything was possible and you wanted to be an astronaut, a policewoman, a scientist, a dancer, or a soccer player. Whatever it was, go back to that state of being and allow yourself to dream wild. As soon as my clients tap into this, beautiful things reappear. Things like the joy of singing and dancing, the freedom they love when out in nature, the fun when puzzling and putting all the pieces together, and more. Simplicities are brought forth. They realise they don't need much to be happy. Again, these dreams don't always have to be "big" or have anything to do with cars, money, handbags and whatsoever.

Unless, of course, that is your dream. If that's the case, then go for it, girl! It's also important to mention that channelling your inner child doesn't mean being childish and not being smart about life. Rather, it means to embrace childlike qualities, like staying curious to learn and remain open for inspiration to come into your life. But, more often than not, these dreams are about the joy of life, which will be unlocked after embracing all three energies: the masculine, the feminine and the inner child energy.

Here's an example of how I tap into all three energies when it comes to working with clients in my business. The structure and drive come with my masculine energy. I have fixed coaching days that are solely for client work. Other days of the week may be for marketing only, podcast recordings, offer development or CEO days. Having this structure in place allows me to be most efficient in my work and it provides me with the guardrails to pour my feminine energy into sessions and days I need to be creative. Furthermore, I put rituals in place that fuel my personal energy so I can show up as my best when working with clients. These would include meditations, more breaks on the day or energy cleanses to really get into a zone of focus, intention, flow, and joy. And I honour my inner child simply with experimenting in sessions, to have fun and fully be present with my client. Or I would have little dance sessions, goof around with my boyfriend, play with the cats, or I have a cheeky doughnut or dessert to celebrate something. Whatever brings me joy and happiness so I can be at my best for myself and others.

The best way to go about these three energies is to do a little audit in a specific area in life that you want to change. Maybe, your goal centres around business, money, health, or relationships, or career. Regardless of what the area is, you can ask yourself the following prompts to get a better understanding of how your masculine, feminine, and inner child energy can support you *and* up-level your experience of life in general.

Exercise: Mini Energy Audit

- *In which moments are you too much in one energy only?*

- *What areas could use more masculine/feminine/inner child energy?*

- *Where do you currently feel most stuck, and how could playing with these energies help you to get unstuck?*

- *What did you do and how did you feel when you had a peak experience, and everything went exactly the way you imagined?*

Masculine Energy Prompts:

- *What structure do you need to put in place to keep going?*

- *What motivates you to do your best? What is your ultimate goal?*

- *What milestones do you want to reach along the way?*

Feminine Energy Prompts:

- *How can you celebrate reaching the milestones and, of course, the goal itself?*

- *When you feel low on energy, what are the best ways for you to recharge?*

- *What fuels your creativity and inspiration?*

Inner Child Energy Prompts:

- *What is something that sparks pure joy within you?*

- *What can you do to make yourself laugh the loudest?*

- *Who can you connect with to do something together?*

For each of these prompts, tap into your intuition and choose one action that best represents this energy. Whether this is a new routine in the morning, singing in the shower more often, or to crack more jokes that you find so funny you get teary eyes. Actions that are in tune with these energies will help you make the most progress toward changing your life. Commit to doing this for the next thirty days, or more and feel free to find a symbol or picture that best represents this energy for you (like fire, water, and rainbow) so you have a visual reminder.

Chapter Summary

This chapter was a whopper, but incredibly powerful. We activated and explored your inner strengths in the form of your best self and allies that you can call upon at any point in time, whenever you need them. The thing is, my dear, you always already had these strengths. You merely had to consciously reawaken them. You also learned how to start embodying these strengths, but there is even more to it, which we will explore in the next chapter.

Chapter 8: Embodying Your New Identity

Walk the walk, girl!

How you see yourself and who you identify as has a huge impact on what you do, how you feel, what you think and how you do, or don't, reach your goals. Which is why the next key step in my Mindset Mastery Framework is identity, or in other words embodiment. Perhaps you view yourself as shy, timid, and incompetent, and therefore at work, you fail to reach your career goals. You are so afraid of speaking up and rarely use your voice. Versus if you consider yourself an expert at what you do, you are more likely to be engaged in meetings and the first to raise your hand for new projects to keep that picture of yourself alive. In this chapter, we will explore in greater detail the immense power that your perception about yourself has. I promise, this is going to be juicy!

When I started out as a Leadership and Mindset Coach in 2021, I had to undergo a huge identity shift myself. Up until then, I only knew of myself as a Corporate Finance Professional, and I had no problem with saying "*I am a Senior Finance Business Partner*". This was a title that was given to me, and I simply accepted it as my truth. However, as I started my coaching training, I obviously began shifting my profession. And yet, for some reason it was so much harder to say "*I am a Coach*", let alone to say "*I'm a business owner and CEO or Founder*". Despite absolutely being in love and obsessed with coaching from day one, it took me months to truly see myself as a Coach. Some of it had to do with the fact that I just started out. How could I possibly call myself a fully fledged Coach if I had only just finished coaching training? Even after finishing, I still wouldn't give myself permission to truly own this new identity. My saboteurs' game was strong! They paired up with Imposter Syndrome and gave me a truly hard time.

Even when fellow coaching colleagues told me, "*Josi, you're an amazing coach!*" I had a tough time believing them and accepting what they said as my truth. What got me out of this was the continuous practice of putting myself out there and keeping on introducing myself as a coach, and of course, also coaching more people. I changed my title on all social platforms and my email footer and started to proudly announce to the whole world "*Hey, I'm a Certified Leadership and Mindset Coach!*", I finally started to truly embody being one. You see, it's not only the repeated affirmation of "I *am a Coach*", but also experiencing it. This powerful combination of affirming and embodiment is what helps your brain to fully integrate that identity shift.

I'm not going to lie: to this day, I have reminder post-it notes on my wall saying "*I am a masterful coach*", just in case my saboteurs poke doubt through my new identity. And that's fine; it's human nature to feel doubtful. But I can now proudly say that I am strong and confident in introducing myself at networking events as a Leadership and Mindset Coach. Because that's who I am. During those last two years I also adopted further identities that I didn't expect at first, which included: entrepreneur, CEO, author, creator, strategist, or even graphic designer (though I wouldn't put that on my CV). What I am working on embodying right now is being a seven-figure business owner and a mum. Whilst transparently, I haven't achieved either of these yet, but we are well on the way. Every day I channel my "seven-figure business owner best self" to show up as her now. It's about becoming her to take the action that will create the new reality.

This process is also called manifestation. If that's not your thing, and you are already calling woo-woo, try and stay open to this concept before labelling it and writing it off. This, too, is a mindset shift, by the way. It's called a growth mindset. I will make sure that it's not too woo-woo so that you can get a good grasp of it as well.

Be—Do—Have

Normally, people would think that if you have a hell of a lot of money due to the work you do, you are a millionaire. Put differently, you "have, do, then be". However, this is not really how things work. When it comes to embodiment, it is all about being first. When you become your desire, you will have the outcome. Therefore, the correct order is: "be, do, then have".

Let's return to the example at the beginning: If you identify as a couch potato (be), you sit on the sofa and eat snacks (do), and your reality is that you might be unhealthy and slightly overweight (have). If you identify yourself as a runner (even if until now you were a couch potato), you will get off that sofa and go for a jog to match that identification. In turn, our reality will be that you feel healthy, lose weight, and make friends at the runners' club in your city.

Through embodiment (which combines be and do), you are also leading by example. You are the change that you want to see in this world. You are the one walking the talk. You are a doer, a player on the field, and not just someone watching from the side-lines, wishing, waiting, and commenting on other people playing. You are in it. Actually, you *are* it. Replace "it" with whatever it is that you want to make real or stand for in this world.

If you want to write a book, start identifying yourself as an author (even if that book isn't written yet). If you want to be an entrepreneur, start that side hustle and decide on a biz name. If you want to be an ice skater, start ice skating. And let this be said, too: It's never too late! There is this incredible story out there of a women who picked up ice skating at the age of 60+ (if I remember correctly) because it was her childhood dream. However, she never before thought that ice skating was *"for people like her"*. I've read about another powerhouse woman who started weightlifting at over 70 because she wanted to become a healthy and fit grandmother. The fact is that both of these women had played small for all these years, they held back until they couldn't ignore their calling any longer. So they gave it a go. They shifted their identity from *"people like them not being able to do these things"* to *"I am an ice skater"* or *"I am a strong old gran!"*. This ultimately lead to them shifting their reality. They decided there and then to embrace their true identity that was aligned with their values, and they started taking action towards their desired reality.

You might think to yourself, *"Well, that's easier said than done. How do I embody my true identity? What exactly do I need to do?"* I was thinking about this question more often than I'd like to admit. But, all my braining finally got me answers, which I will share with you in the next pages.

The Power of Visualisation

The easiest way to embody your dream is through visualisation. In fact, even athletes use visualisation to prepare themselves for the run, the fight, the swim, the climb, or the slope down the hill. They simply visualise themselves winning. In their minds' eyes, they see themselves running the marathon. They envision the feeling of their feet touching the ground, how the air feels when it fills their lungs and the emotions they will experience when they finally cross the finish line. Or, they see the route they are climbing upwards, smell and feel the chalk on their hands, and tap into the sensation of reaching the edge from which they enjoy the best view ever. This practice fuels our motivation and primes you for the actual action for when it's time. But, that's not all. Research has shown that even envisioning training your muscles and doing a full workout in your mind, feeling every rep, can stimulate muscle growth (Ranganathan et al., 2004). Of course, this does not ever replace a regular training session. But, it reveals that the mind is incredibly powerful and can influence your reality in ways that you have been closed off to until now.

I have my very own example of this during weightlifting. I like playing with my mind every now and then just to see the difference in the impact it can have. When I try to do another personal best (or a one-maximum repetition), and I just go through the motions, I'm more likely to fail the attempt than when I envision myself prior as succeeding at it. I often include another mini visualisation, in which I imagine sending a lot of energy to my legs and powering them up. Despite having just failed that same weight before, I am now able to lift it. I didn't grow any more muscle in those five minutes, I just simply changed my mindset and embodied a stronger self. If you regularly work out, try this practice for yourself and take note of the incredible results.

This doesn't solely work for any physical activities, of course. This powerful visualisation works for succeeding in other situations or challenges, too. For example, you can try to visualise your important work meeting tomorrow going extremely well. Or, you see yourself making new connections at the networking event. Maybe you imagine yourself being in total flow when batch-recording your next three to five podcast episodes. If your dream is to become a world-famous public speaker you may envision yourself stepping confidently on stage to do your first ever Ted Talk. Begin picturing yourself doing the things that your aspirational identity would do. The more you do it, the more you will realise that you start to become that best version of yourself. The key here is to do it regularly. This is not a "I do it once and never again type of thing". The more often you do it, the better the results will be.

This is why I have integrated visualisation practices in my meditation rituals before I fall asleep. There are many different ways to do this, so find what gels best with you. Maybe it's a three-minute visualisation here, a short journal there, or talking with a friend about it and dreaming together.

Exercise: The Embodiment Walk

This exercise has been one of my staples for years. I first started doing it in Finland when I came across the book "*The Secret*" by Rhonda Byrne. This is when I started to dive extremely deep into anything to do with manifesting. Or, you could just say that I became obsessed with it (I maybe still am). When I was in Finland, I lived slightly outside of Helsinki, so I had an incredible beach and forest area right at my doorstep that just screamed for regular walks. My daily practice included going for one to two daily, thirty-to-sixty-minute walks. During these walks I would envision myself applying for my dream job and moving to the UK. Every time, I got more detailed. I even knew what my exact job title would be and "*I see myself as a Finance Business Partner*" I would say to myself, "*I see myself living in a house in the UK*". Even though there were at first zero opportunities in the UK, and it almost seemed impossible to get a role over there, I kept on visualising myself as a Finance Business Partner and moving to the UK. And I kid you not, it didn't take too long until that opening popped up as an email in my inbox, I applied, and the rest is history.

To make this embodiment and manifestation walk even more effective, you might even go into an area that your aspirational identity would be in. Maybe she loves to shop in expensive stores, so go to that street and imagine that you are buying all of the things you see in the windows. Or, go inside and try some things on. It's not about buying anything and spending money you don't currently have, but about normalising this feeling if this is what you desire. If you would love to live in a specific area and have a dream house in mind, go for a walk there and imagine how it would be to live here. Think about where you would get your groceries, and where you would drink your morning coffee. And you can start with just the affirmation, "*I see myself as the woman who* _____ *and* _____." (fill in the blanks). Just start walking as that exact woman you aspire to be. You might notice that you walk a little more proud, or there is a spring to your step. You may feel lighter, or perhaps you notice the warmth of the sunshine on your skin. This is how you do embodiment, and provide your brain with the experience of "what if…" which it will store as additional proof that this new reality is possible for you.

As I mentioned before, embodiment is also leading by example and embodying the change that you want to see in this world. Embodiment is walking the talk and not just saying that you are doing XYZ, but truly showcasing that you are living it. This is especially important to fellow business owners. Even more so for coaches. It's so easy to just tell others what to do or what you are doing, because how on earth could you be demonstrating how you work on your mindset for example?

131

Working on your mindset is not an overnight kind of game. It takes a while because you have to train your brain to think in ways that it hasn't before. But, people will notice. They will notice the change in the tone of your voice as you speak with more confidence during the meeting. They will notice the shift in your posture as you stand up a little taller as you speak in front of your audience. They will notice you fidgeting less, speaking up more, sharing your opinion, and speaking louder. They notice the subtle shifts in your being that you might not see at first. Thus, the best way to embody and lead by example when it comes to mindset shifts is to again, just become that new version.

Then one day people might come around and ask you, "*Damn, how did you get so confident?*" You can then give them this book and say, "*Well, this book has taught me the basics. You should give it a read, too.*" Joke aside, but you can tell them this: do the embodiment walk anywhere and everywhere. Literally. Always put on your best-self-suit before you do anything and show up as her. Again, (broken record alarm), the more you do it, the more you will indeed become that best version of yourself.

A Note on Outgrowing Others

As you evolve into this new version, I want to let you know that you might very likely find that some of your relationships will improve, but you will also outgrow others that have been a part of your life for a long time. You might even find you are absolutely not aligned with them any more and either get into arguments or simply seek distance to them. This is completely normal. And whilst it might be sad at first, it is also an opportunity for you to spend more time with people who either love you no matter how much you grow and change or are aligned with you at this next level. Surround yourself with people who will inspire you to reach even further. Anyone you meet in life is meant to be there for a certain period of time.

If they are meant to stay, they will. But if they are meant to leave, trust your intuition and set the both of you free to go on separate growth-journeys.

Instead of focusing solely on the loss, focus on the good times you had together (or the lessons you learned) and be grateful for them. It's quite similar to hanging onto your favourite pair of jeans that has too many holes in it or simply doesn't fit your style any more. You love them, but they're not for you any more. The empowered version of yourself knows and appreciates this and learns to let go.

I don't think that I've ever had one client who did not outgrow others, including friends, family and now ex-husbands. But also, none of these women regrets her growth one single bit and instead celebrates her newfound happiness within herself and the upgraded relationships around her. You will have better and deeper conversations with others and handle arguments with a lot more grace. But you will also inspire others to become their best version of themselves. By oozing this new energy, being on that high-vibe frequency, striving for your dreams, and living your best life ever, you inspire others to do the same or attract like minded people into your life. You will become a living example of what's possible. In turn, you will inspire others to become empowered, all because you chose to live for yourself, to be happy, and to trust you can do tough shit. It's the kind of domino effect you *do* want to have.

Chapter Summary

Embodiment is the most powerful action you can take to shift your identity and therefore create a new reality for yourself. It is the next step on the journey of "change starts from within", and it is an extension of you working on and shifting your mindset. You now know several ways to shift your identity, and you also know how it will change your reality. Through embodiment, you cover both the "be" and the "do" in order to "have". Which is why this step truly deserves its own chapter. However, in the grand scheme of things, it is simply one of many actions you can "do" to get closer and closer to your "have", which is what we will unpack in the next chapter.

Chapter 9: Taking Action and Building Strong Habits

Three rules that are stuck on a sticky note on my wall:

1. *If you don't go after what you want, you will never get it.*
2. *If you don't ask, the answer will always be no.*
3. *If you don't step forward, you will remain at the same place.*

With the last point of the previous chapter, we already introduced the basic concept of inspired action. As a reminder, it is any action or way of doing something as that is aligned with your best self, or is the way she would handle it. In this chapter, we take a closer look at actions in general, and more importantly, how to form habits that are of service to you and bring you closer to your goals and aspirational identity.

Actions are the external expression of your mind in the form of actively doing something or getting into motion. Working on your mindset and doing the inner work is half of your new success story. Actually getting your hands dirty is the other half. Whilst the thoughts you had or the decisions you made in your mind have been the cause, the things you do is the effect. There is no real change if you continue doing the same thing, even if you think differently. Consequently, we cannot just leave this part of the equation untouched. Which is why "Action" and "Habits" have their own link in my signature framework, the Mindset Mastery Roadmap. They are the key drivers that actually lead to the "have" we desire. They also are key in any change of program you want to pursue, as this is how you collect the proof your brain needs to accept the new program.

The simplest way to tap into inspired action is to ask yourself the following questions:

- *What do I need to do to get where I want to be?*

- *What decisions would I make based on where I want to be?*

- *Who do I need to become and how do I become her?*

These questions may uncover answers to big projects and can unveil solutions to daily tasks. As we previously explored, exemplify the power by asking specific allies or your leader within, "*Hey, how would you handle this? What would you do?*".

Another powerful way is through unlocking the power of your intuition. And I dare say, I wouldn't be where I am today without listening to and trusting my intuition. Let's travel back into the year 2021, which was my big year where everything changed. It was the year that I got married, and shortly after broke up and started the annulment process. My intuition had been screaming at me like crazy leading up to the wedding. My inner voice was begging me not to go through with it. However, my saboteurs were so strong that I could not adjust my path until after the event. The curtains dropped in front of my eyes, leaving me with a big, fat "*FUCK!*" floating over my head.

Luckily, as soon as I could finally see one clear path in front of me, which was *out*, that's where I aimed my focus.

I don't know if I can even describe how I felt once those chains and ties were finally severed. My body was just flooded with relief, I could breathe again, the air smelled nicer, food tasted better. It was as though I boosted my experience of life with just one decision. I enjoyed my own company, and finally felt like myself again. My mind was fully fixated on doing whatever I wanted. I decided that I was going to live my single life for a while. I 100% was not looking for a new relationship, as I had just broken out and rediscovered my wings. But the universe had different plans for me.

One day, I woke up to the urgent thought in my mind to download Tinder. Yes, you read that right. My intuition was screaming at me once again, and because I now knew exactly how it felt, I couldn't resist. (Side-note: when your intuition screams at you, it feels like a huge force pulling and guiding you towards doing something that may have not even been on your radar at all. It hits you out of the blue. Suddenly, it is the biggest no-brainer that you ever experienced and there is only one way to stop it from screaming: you do the thing).

I downloaded Tinder and got scrolling. Holy Cow! I was immediately overwhelmed by all of the swiping, I didn't like the concept at all, it was too superficial for me, but I continued trusting my intuition and kept on swiping, mostly left. In fact, I swiped left so much that Tinder sent me a notification that they had to increase the range as they were running out of men closer by. After a marathon of swiping, I matched with five people. Three of them, I unmatched again after a couple days of chatting. Another one shortly after, leaving me with one guy. I really enjoyed chatting to him; there was a lovely flow in the conversation and that was the exact motto I agreed upon with my best self: *"Go with the flow"*. As time went on, this man was ticking more and more boxes on my list of must-haves and must-not-haves for a potential new partner. I'm not going to lie, but there was a tiny tug of war between my best self and my saboteurs. Whilst (to my surprise!) my best self continued saying *"just go with it, trust your intuition, trust what feels good right now."* My saboteurs responded with, *"It's too early. What is this slutty behaviour? You're not even through the annulment papers yet."* Every time this happened, I took a deep breath and continued following my intuition. So, I met up with this all-boxes-ticking-man, and our first date was just incredible. It was full of flow, fun, and ease. I had never felt like this before. There was no need "to perform" or to come across a certain way. I could just be myself and I felt safe. Long story short, this wonderful man and I have been in an over two-year relationship at the point of writing this chapter. And I couldn't be happier. All thanks to a sudden intuition-thunderstruck, followed by keeping on checking in with my intuition, and doing the do.

I'm telling you this story in the hope that you can see where taking inspired action and trusting your intuition can lead you. Whilst one of humanity's greatest gifts is the brain and logical thinking, this gut instinct is something we need to re-learn how to trust. It is so full of wisdom and guidance that our logical brain, which is basing everything on experience, memories and facts simply cannot fathom. Yes, it can make predictions, but that's a logical way of going about things, not an intuitive way. You can imagine it like feelers of an insect.

Tapping into your intuition gives you clarity as to what is the right or wrong way to go and what actions you need to take to get there.

Now, I would argue that not all actions will be completely intuitive or inspired, but they will give you a great indication for action steps you have to take in general to live a life in fulfilment. Whilst they can absolutely be both at the same time, I personally see them more as the kick-off action for other stepping stones to follow, which have more of a habitual and/or intentional nature. What do I mean by this exactly?

Well, many of my clients have big goals like writing books, building a community, or becoming a public speaker to name a few. If we take the latter as an example, the main reasons why they want to achieve this is to have an even bigger positive impact on others, to be seen and recognised as the expert in their field. If you remember, the key to getting this change started is to have a reason (your "Why") and to then decide what exactly you want to achieve through setting a goal and how you want to feel whilst doing so through setting an intention. To get there, you need to put in a certain effort, which is the repetitive, habitual action, like hosting events and workshops, taking lessons in public speaking to practise, and learn being comfortable in front of the camera and audiences. The action of starting this process and deciding to use some time out of your day to one day stand on the stage and hold your first Ted Talk is the inspired action. What follows is building habits.

Habits are, for good reason, a key element of my Mindset Mastery Roadmap. What we do on a daily basis is what creates our identity (remember: couch potato or gym bunny) and that influences our reality, such as how we enjoy and live life. Which is why, in the rest of this chapter I will guide you through some common mistakes I see people make (and that I have made myself) when it comes to consistently taking steps towards their goals. Or in other words: building a new habit.

Mistake 1:
They forget that there are actually two habits to build for one action

If you are wondering what the hell I'm talking about, let's take a closer look at this action: *"I want to sell my services on my stories every day"*. The obvious action is the selling itself. However, the "secret" second action is in showing up to do so. It's the same for drinking a glass of water every morning after getting up; you have to go into the kitchen to drink that water. Or, maybe you want to go outside every day for half an hour. To do so, you have to show up at your doorstep to go outside.

Because people often ignore this secret action that is needed to perform the actual thing, they fail, because they haven't built the habit of showing up yet. They don't know that in order to make a change in their lives, they need to show up for themselves to make it happen.

Solution:

Practise showing up first, to do the things that you set out to do and make it ridiculously simple. That could look like going to the gym, even without the intent to train. I can hear you literally thinking right now: "*But when I do that, I might as well, train?*" Exactly. But also, if you don't, which is totally fine by the way, you at least showed up. And that's what we are practising right now.

In the case of my writing practice, I made it a habit to show up for it in the form of writing every day. At first, it wasn't at the same time and definitely was not with the purpose of writing this book. I just wanted to write. Whether that is a new blogpost, an article on LinkedIn, or an email to my email fam, or just simply journaling in my notebook. For the last four years, not one day went by when I didn't write. So when it came to really rolling up my sleeves and showing up to write for this book, I already had that practice and discipline done and dusted.

And if you are thinking right now, "*How on earth do I even get the motivation to show up?*" Go back to your "Why", and remind yourself of your goal. That's your motivation right there. If it doesn't motivate you enough, then you don't want it bad enough to build the discipline needed. So rework it, and in doing so, make it irresistible.

Interesting side fact here: most often, the motivation doesn't come before you do the thing, it comes after you went outside, after you trained, after you had that glass of water. Why? Because it makes you feel better. Because you think, "*Hey, this wasn't that hard and I feel great, and I want to do that again.*" That's what keeps you going. However, it's crucial to not solely rely on motivation but to learn to build the discipline for the days you just don't feel like getting out of bed and going to the gym or turn on that camera to film yourself.

Mistake 2:
They make the new habit too big or too hard to follow through and get frustrated or impatient

I'm 100% sure that you have been there. You wanted to change up your whole routine, made big plans, stuck with it for two to three days, got exhausted, missed a day, and then dropped it because you couldn't be bothered any more, as it was just too hard. Or, you started a new habit, managed to stick with it for a while, but got frustrated because you couldn't see any results. Perhaps you feel like you have plateaued. If you end up in self-sabotage mode, you might then beat yourself up, believing that you are incapable of sticking to change. The issue with this is that you may be making this your reality, and therefore harder for you in general to build a new habit in future because you trained your brain to not follow through.

Solution:

At the end of this chapter, you will probably hate me because I will say this so often: simple is best. Make it easier for you to stick to that habit. Start with one change at a time, break it down into more manageable steps, use accountability structures to keep you going, and celebrate every time you did it. Celebrating can be listening to your favourite song, enjoying a cup of your favourite tea, doing a mini-meditation, or whatever else feels great for you. Having said that, sometimes it can also require drastic action to break through a glass ceiling, but there might not always be an option to do so.

My best example is building a business. It takes time and consistency to get to the juicy part of the J-curve, and you will have to make patience your new best friend deep in the down-curve right before you see the results you envisioned. There simply are no drastic actions that will lead to overnight success, sustainability, and client retention.

Here are two fun ways you can try out to make it easier to stick to one new habit at a time:

Habit Stacking:

What is something you already do every day anyway? For example: Brushing your teeth, having your morning coffee, or cooking dinner. To play this mini game, you affirm that every time *after* you brush your teeth, you will drink a glass of water. Then, after you drink your glass of water, you will put on your gym clothes, and so on.

So, for the action or habit you want to build to live life at a ten, play with this formula:

After I (current habit), I will (new habit).

<u>Pay Yourself:</u>

Create an incentive through paying yourself to follow through with your commitment. Think of something you have wanted to buy for a really long time, but never really felt like the purchase would be justified. That could be a really cool armchair that would be an amazing statement piece in your house, or it may be some artwork of your favourite artist you had your eyes on for years. It could also be a weekend trip that you've wanted to take with your partner for so long. Choose something that excites you and figure out how much money you need to save to get it. Then, decide how much you are going to pay yourself, every time you complete the action.

For example: You want to purchase an armchair, which costs £300. Your goal is to sell your services on Instagram Stories every day. You give yourself at least thirty minutes to do the stories and engage with your community, because you want to reach the right people and build strong bonds with everyone. You decide that every time you do it, you will pay yourself £2. So, overall you will need to show up and do the thing 150x. Any day you skip, prolongs the process of finally getting your armchair. If you do sixty minutes a day because you also write an email or a post to sell, you pay yourself double the amount.

Again, you have full permission to be creative and come up with your own genius idea that keeps you going. I also highly recommend reading James Clear's book *"Atomic Habits"*; it's truly a game changer!

Mistake 3:
They miss a day and don't pick it back up again

For this one, it's first important to understand why you don't pick it up again. Is it because your saboteur took over control and they are saying things like: *"It's too hard to find time to read every night, let's just watch a video tonight and we read again tomorrow!"*, and then tomorrow comes and the saboteur repeats the same excuse. Or, is it because your "Why" isn't strong enough and you don't see the purpose in it? Is it because your priorities have changed and you actually need to prioritise something completely different for now because it would otherwise be too much on your plate?

If it's the first reason: Consult your best self. Would she drop it? No. So, show up again the next day and don't miss twice. (Unless you're ill and you physically can't, don't be too hard on yourself, recover first and then get back at it. Again, we are not aiming for a perfectly crossed out calendar; we aim for consistency).

If it's the second reason: Go back to your "Why", make it stronger, remind yourself of your goal, visualise yourself achieving that goal, bathe in the sensation of reaching it, and refuel your motivation, and build discipline.

146

If it's the third reason: Can you reduce the time it takes to do the action? For example, instead of working out for thirty minutes, do fifteen minutes. Is there something else you can stop doing? You might even want to consult the "Four D's of Time Management Matrix" to find out what you have to 100% do, and what you can delegate, delay, and delete. This frees up your time and energy to focus on the most important aspects of your work and personal life. Consider outsourcing tasks like house cleaning, grocery shopping, or administrative work, if it's feasible for you. Another way could be to use time blocking and chunk similar tasks up into one larger time period. For example, when I create my content plan, I do so in one sitting for the whole month ahead. Or, when writing my bi-weekly newsletter, I will write several in advance rather than on the day.

Of course, the solution that works best for you might even be a combination of all of these or something completely different, but there are ways. You can find a template that will help you with the Four D's and getting your priorities straight on the resource page.

Mistake 4:
They think small steps don't count or contribute to the end goal

The amount of times that people (myself included, by the way), would not recognise the little steps they took every day to get where they are today, is mind-blowing to me. I truly have to hold up my own hand here, because it still is something I have to consciously practise every day, to celebrate and acknowledge also the small steps. This includes showing up every day to write, it includes educating myself with another video on self-publishing, posting on social media, connecting with a client, improving a section on my website, meditating for 3 minutes, putting on a facemask. Like in itself these actions look small and simple. But they all sum up to a better work-life blend, high-level self-care, finishing this book, a strong and healthy body, an engaged community and happy clients.

Solution:

Make every step you take count, small or big. Whether you take a "pebble-stone step" or jump over a rock, they all count towards you reaching the peak of that mountain. You can even go as far and put one thing only for the day onto your to-do list. And then celebrate the heck out of achieving that. Everything else you get done that day is a bonus, but you most definitely got the most important thing out of the way, and that's what counts. It also will take a lot of pressure off your shoulders and you don't get hung up in the "Overdoer" mentality. If you like visual proof like ticking a box or crossing out the calendar, you can also put your actions or milestones onto post-it notes on your wall. Every time you complete the action or reach the goal, you can take it down. Combine it with ideas for how you want to reward yourself so you don't forget to celebrate your amazing accomplishment.

Mistake 5:
They only focus on the outcome or goal alone

Now this one is an interesting one. I'm sure you have heard of the saying *"Go at it with the end in mind"* (or something similar). I do highly recommend always having your goal and your vision in sight so you don't lose track. However, focusing solely on that, might also lead to frustration if things turn out slightly differently than you expected. Or they attach too much meaning to reaching that goal and fall into the trap of *"I will only feel better/accomplished/happy/proud/xyz when I have achieved this"*. Maybe you think you can only be happy when yo have found your dream partner, rather than focusing on being happy in the present moment. Or that you have to be married by a certain age and start panicking as you get closer or succeed your self-inflicted "deadline". What happens here, is that you don't acknowledge the journey and what you do have already in your life. It's a lack mentality to be in. Think about it this way, you don't go hiking to only enjoy the view from the top of the mountain, you go hiking because you like doing it.

Solution:

Yes, be obsessed with your goal, but also be obsessed with the process of getting there. Fall in love with the practice, adore your schedule that will enable you to achieve that specific outcome. If you make the process your goal, you already are a winner. You don't need to have your dream partner by your side to know that you're a great catch. If you learn to build an incredible relationship with yourself and how to love yourself first you will enjoy the process of eventually finding you dream match, rather than clinging onto this "must-have" in order to be happy. Romanticise your life, take yourself out on dates, and make practising self-love a non-negotiable every single day. Love what you do, so you do what you love.

In the resource page of this book you will find a habit workbook to help you build and track your new habits and routines that are based on who you want to become and where you want to be.

Mistake 6: They don't set themselves up for success

What I mean by this is that often times, people forget to adapt their physical environment to support the new habit, or reduce the instinct to gravitate to the old habit. Take learning a new language for example. You want to learn the mother tongue of your partner so you can communicate better with their family. But you don't ever use it in your day-to-day life and have little to no exposure to it besides the daily 10-minute Duolingo lessons you take on your phone. You might have heard of the saying that the best way to use a language is to to be where it's spoken. No of course this might not be always possible, but there are ways to immerse yourself even more in that language, even without travelling. Another example of this would be: if you want to nourish your body with healthy, balanced meals, yet you always keep a stack of crisps, chocolate and other sweets around. You know that if they are there, you will eat them, yet you hold onto them anyway. Or, your desk is always messy and packed with all sorts of things, causing you to grow distracted when sitting down or having to clean up first. Perhaps it might be that you always keep your phone close by, and despite wanting to quickly research something on it, you somehow got sucked into the never-ending TikTok scroll. Maybe you're on your fifth YouTube video that has nothing to do with the actual topic you first searched.

Solution:

Change your environment to suit your new endeavours. Get rid of the snacks and replace them with easily accessible healthier ones. Watch your favourite shows in the language you want to learn or change the language set up in your phone. Put your gym clothes out the night before. Clean up the desk every day to prepare it for the next day. Put your phone into the room next door, lock it away, or use apps like "Forest" (personal recommendation from my side, as I use it for every writing session). Do whatever it is that you must do in order to make this new habit as easy as possible. At the same time, make it as challenging as possible to engage with the old one.

Exercise: Build Powerful Habits

A great method to find out which new habits you should build, and which old habits you may want to change or stop completely, is a habit self-assessment. For this exercise, write down everything you do on a regular basis, starting with getting up, brushing your teeth, being on the phone, etc. Be brutally honest with yourself. This is not to judge you, but to hold up the mirror and see where you might be wasting time and energy on habits that don't actually serve you. You might even audit your activities for a whole week for more accuracy as what you do might change from day-to-day.

Once you have this list, mark every habit with either a "+" for a good habit, a "-" for a bad habit, and an "x" for a neutral habit. Then, you can use this insight to either introduce a new habit that you want to stack upon existing ones (reminder: follow the habit stacking formula) or replace an old, bad habit with a new one.

To prevent yourself from changing up your entire routine, only select one to three action steps that you will take from now on consistently. Write them down and note as to why these habits are important to you. Include how they will contribute to you reaching your goal. Last, but not least, decide on a method of tracking that will keep you going. Whether it is a simple checklist, red crosses in your calendar, the paper-clip method, post-its, or paying yourself, choose what works best for you and seems the most exciting and effective.

If I were to recommend one habit to build to every human on this planet it would be this: Exercise regularly. Reason being: this is a keystone habit. These habits are the strategic habits that trigger a chain reaction of positive behaviour in other areas of our lives. Identifying and focusing on these keystone habits can accelerate our progress towards success. The benefit of regular exercise is not only on a physiological level, meaning that you get healthy and fit. The benefits of movement also have a massive impact on your mental health. And I'm not only talking about the serotonin influx post-workout, but reduced anxiety, depression, increased self-esteem, and cognitive function. In other words, it provides you with more energy to do other things in life better and feel less sluggish. However, it is also one of the easiest and quickest ways to break out of the self-sabotaging cycle. When you find yourself in a bad mood, triggered, or in saboteur-mode, after you acknowledge what is going on, get moving. Go for a short walk, do a couple sun-salutations, anything to disrupt your current thought process. If you have disabilities or chronic health conditions, please consult with your personal doctor for specific exercises that you can do which may include more gentle stretches or breathing exercises. This way you tick two boxes in one go, you train your brain to overcome the saboteur and you move your body, win-win for self-care!

What I also want to point out is the sheer power of consistent small steps. Yes, they might not seem like much over time, but as you continue taking them day after day, session after session, you might look back and find that your whole life has completely changed. This is exactly what my client Lara did, and this is only the beginning!

Lara is one of the clients who started working with me when I just started out as a coach. She has been working with me for years and her main goals at the beginning were to find happiness and fulfilment in her relationship and career. As we were working together, Lara turned her entire life around. But she had to put in a lot of work to get there. Her biggest self-sabotage types were the critic and people-pleaser. She was quick to attach her worth onto others and what others thought of her. Her pet peeve was to give all of her time to others rather than focusing it on her own needs and refilling her own cup. This made it quite clear that the main theme we got to work on was all about her learning to put herself first, to trust herself fully, and know that she can lean on her own powers. We started with implementing regular self-care practices and having honest conversations with others. Of course, there were many trials and errors, but Lara had incredible results. We linked one inspired action after the other, built strong habits that supported her and her goals. Lara was making fast progress. The key for her to stay accountable for the actions was that her vision was, and still is, so clear. She knows what she wants, and she knows that she will get it. It's the fuel to keep her going, even when times get tough.

During our time together Lara left her toxic relationship, let go of friends that she outgrew, and up-levelled her career. Whilst in the beginning we worked on smaller shifts and improvements, over time, Lara reached a level of self-awareness that made bigger jumps possible. This is the compound effect of change and consistent actions. It all adds up, and the result is a woman who knows her powers and doesn't shy away from holding up the mirror to continue working on herself and get what she wants.

A Word of Caution About "Shoulding"

"Shoulding" is the art of deciding on action steps that you think you *should* do, potentially because you saw someone else is doing it and having success with it. This might especially be the case whenever you're still learning a lot about that new endeavour of yours. Just to give you an example from the point of view of building a business: there are *thousands* of ways to build a business. You can try countless models, strategies, templates, checklists, courses, etc. Being flooded with all this insight makes it very easy to stray away from your current strategy and think, "*Oh this person is offering lots of smaller trainings and courses, I should do that too.*" It can also be the other way around and sound like, "*This person doesn't do different workshops every month, maybe I shouldn't do that either.*" These are all thoughts that I have had countless times on the journey of building my business. This thinking trap is called "Shoulding", and is caused by "Comparisonitis". Whilst there is nothing wrong with getting inspiration from others, we should avoid continuously second-guessing ourselves. Not leading with intuition can decrease our self-trust. Yes, if your strategy is shit and you have proof it isn't working or going anywhere, then of course, adapt it. Take time to analyse what others are doing right and get inspired to create your own action plan that is uniquely your own. But, take all of these "shoulds" with a grain of salt, and observe how often you voice them. Take notice of how frequently you feel the need to switch things up or look outwards to find advice.

Chapter Summary

In this chapter, you have learned about the importance of (inspired) action, what it means, and how proper action steps will lead to your desired outcome. We've also debunked some of the biggest mistakes when it comes to building habits. Therefore, you're well-equipped to build your very own routine of life-mastery.

Chapter 10: The Secret to Self-Care

Taking a break is one of the most underrated productivity hacks ever!

This chapter is very close to my heart and is something that I strongly felt deserved an entire chapter so that the words could breathe. This whole book can be seen as one bible for self-care, as all of these practices that you are learning are looking after yourself on levels around your mind, body, heart, and soul. Whilst I'm obviously a strong advocate for putting in the work and all the doing, I also know how easy it is to do too much. And yes, you *can* do too much if you either hate or love what you do. The fact that you're working doesn't change.

And in a world where being constantly busy and productive, rather than effective, is highly praised, it is so important to continue reminding ourselves that rest and recharging are not the villains in our story.

They actually are some of our biggest supporters, and this chapter will show you why. Before we dive in, I want to share with you a little more about my burnout experience. Most importantly, the symptoms that I was experiencing. Because noticing them early can help protect you from getting a full blast of absolute exhaustion. The thing with burnout is that it starts slow. It sneaks up on you. One day you feel like you have everything under control. People are celebrating you for doing it all, and are also wondering, *"How the heck is she doing it all?"* The next day, you plummet into a hole, questioning why you can't deal with a simple task like writing an email, or even getting out of bed any more. All the years of hustling, grinding, and pushing through are finally catching up and your body and mind simply cannot deal with it any more.

At its peak, a regular day for me looked like this: waking up after a sleepless night; dreading opening the laptop; skipping the workout because I had zero energy (physically, mentally and spiritually); having breakfast and lunch at my desk to get the work done; at the same time, struggling to get any work done; getting into my head about it and breaking down, tears dripping on the keyboard whilst more and more emails and messages pop up in the group chat; ending the day feeling like shit and ruminating in bed about everything I have to do, reiterating over and over again that it's all too much for me to handle. It felt like all the colours disappeared out of my life and I became even more of a hermit, closed off and easily agitated. It felt like a dementor from the Harry Potter books constantly sucked all of the joy out of my life.

What got me out of it was my determination. I knew that I deserved better than this. At some point, I simply couldn't stand it any longer and knew that I had to change something and take control. I started voicing my struggles to my managers and colleagues. But at first, not much help came from that side. I had to really put my foot down in order to get me off of the project that was causing the biggest workload for me. The other cause was working on my mindset and getting myself out of my mindset funk. I needed to shift my belief that I'm only worthy/good enough/loveable if I work my ass off and function like a superhuman with three brains and eight arms.

The biggest shift, however, which ultimately got me out of burnout and back into a thriving and happy place was this: I didn't just put more self-care on my to-do list. I made it my number one priority and a non-negotiable. And it still is, to this day.

Burnout has taught me many things. Despite it being an incredibly shitty experience, it also changed my life around. The beauty of hindsight of this period in my life is that I 100% know that I will never go back. But luckily, I now know how I can prevent it from happening again. And if you are thinking, "But Josi, you now work for yourself and love what you do, so surely that means you won't burn out again!" Think again. It's actually an even bigger balancing act when coming out of the nine-to-five and plunging into the entrepreneurial world to do what you love doing. Because you might very well end up working twenty-four-seven. And whilst yes, if you love what you do, it may feel less like work. But, the underlying fact that you are still w-o-r-k-i-n-g, is nevertheless the same.

Many fellow business owners actually end up working more and experience stronger feelings of guilt, FOMO, and anxiety when leaving the business alone for a day (most of them don't even dare to take off weeks). There are many reasons as to why this is happening. One being the fact that we trained ourselves for years to constantly work. Even though we may have chosen to build our own business for more free time freedom, it doesn't mean that we immediately change the old behaviours and beliefs in the process.

Another reason is the fact that now, we are a one-woman-shop. We are the CEO, Marketing Director, Salesperson, Graphic Designer, Website Developer, Coach, Mentor, Accountant, Tech Support, Customer Service, and so much more. In the beginning phase, there is no one else to rely on other than ourselves, so the fear of lacking behind and not making enough sales when taking time off, is real. For me too.

I do have a well-working burnout-symptoms-radar and am pretty good with sticking to my boundaries and my self-care practices. However, I still get the occasional nudge from my partner to remind me when I slide into over-working habits or get distracted during a workout because a client just messaged me. Which Brings Us to the Number One Self-Care Practice:

Setting Boundaries

Boundaries are a wonderfully misunderstood thing. Most people find them selfish, but I say otherwise. They are one of the most beneficial practices, not only for your own good, but also for other people's good. They protect your energy and peace, and people get to always enjoy you at your best. I don't know about you, but I would rather collaborate with someone who is well rested, energised, passionate and ready to have a conversation, over someone who barely slept because they were doing overtime the day before, is on the fourth cup of coffee, and is distracted by the constant pinging of their chat because they need to multitask.

Due to the misconceptions of boundaries, and being programmed to believe that they make you bitchy, bossy, or distant, many people struggle with setting them. Yet, not setting them can come at a high cost. Not only are you putting yourself at the mercy of others and giving your power away, but you may also feel disrespected, taken advantage of, depleted of energy, or even passive-aggressive. All of this can be avoided through setting boundaries. And no, doing so does not make you a bitch or mean or anything else. That right there is your saboteur talking, not your empowered best self. Struggling to set boundaries does come from self-sabotage types like the People-Pleaser, Overdoer, or even Victim Player. And in the last chapters, you learned how to spot them and overcome them.

Nonetheless, I want to share with you three key elements that will help you set strong self-care boundaries so that you never again struggle with finding the time to take care of yourself.

1. Transparent Communication of the Boundary

It shouldn't be of any news to you that no one on this planet can read minds. You might have a boundary internally, but rarely communicate them. You may find yourself complaining to others about how your mum once again showed up at your door without telling you, even though you just wanted to hop into a nice hot bath. Yes, it might be scary having to tell your mum, "Listen, you can't show up without an invitation, I have plans. If you want to spend time together, let's agree on a time next time." But you may be surprised by how often people welcome your honesty. If they love you unconditionally, it's no problem at all and there's no need to fear rejection. If they do make a fuss about it, then it's their problem and it doesn't mean that you need to over-explain why. There's no need to tell them all of the reasons why you want to set the boundary, even if they don't understand. A solid, "No," can already be enough of a boundary. The important part is in voicing it.

2. Choose an Appropriate Consequence

When you communicate your boundary, make sure that you also communicate a consequence the other person will want to avoid from happening. Also, if they still overstep your boundary, don't shy away from making that consequence become reality. How you treat your boundaries is how you teach others to treat you.

Let's return to the example of unwanted visits from your mum. If you communicate your boundary, yet she still shows up at your door saying, "It can't possibly be such a bad thing if a parent wants to see their kid now and then," be firm with the consequence. Don't let her in and send her back home. The next time you are free and choose to spend quality time with her, she will appreciate it more, because you will be present with her. When the boundaries are learned to be respected by both ends, it creates a more harmonious and balanced relationship.

3. No Exceptions

If you continue rescheduling your me-time, amending the boundaries, or making exceptions here and there, do you even have a boundary in place? Stand behind your word, and don't fear putting firm boundaries in place that you commit to respecting. Because in the end, respecting your boundaries is respecting yourself.

Even with all of the things on your to-do list, make sure that you prioritise time for self-care and protect it by strong boundaries. Because the thing is, if you don't get to rest and recharge, you have no energy to do neither of the things you have to do, nor the things you love to do. Which is why it's so crucial to focus on your wellbeing when you feel like you've hit rock bottom. It's the only way to get your energy back up and deal with everything else. Only then can you expand on your self-care. Self-care needs to be of utmost priority at all times.

Take professional athletes as an example. They are not running marathons twenty-four-seven, nor fully deplete their energy each day. On the contrary, they understand the importance of rest to build muscle. They must recharge to be at their best during the next race. They regulate their stress levels outside of their profession and have strong self-care practices, because they know that fatigue can be the difference between gold and bronze. When striving for the gold medal, self-care needs to be a priority.

Another example would be creatives like painters or writers. They know the importance of stepping away to refuel their creative energy and inspiration. There is a reason why the best ideas happen when you're standing underneath the shower, only caring about how to reach that middle part of your back with the sponge, and then the lightbulb moment suddenly hits you. I, too, get most of my inspiration for posts from going inward or a walk, rather than forcing myself to work harder and harder.

So, you see: rest and recharge are, contrary to popular belief, very productive and effective. This superduo is what helps you build resilience because you can actually persevere for longer.

It's what keeps the candle burning in a sustainable way. Trying to fire it up too much for too long will cause it to extinguish itself, and it's harder to fully light it up again versus tending to the flame.

We as human beings are so well trained to continue working and hustling and being busy all of the time that rest seems counter-intuitive and unnatural. I call it the "Resting Paradox". Of course, we have seen some results with this behaviour, but at what cost? Is burnout worth it? Is being unhappy and feeling unfulfilled worth it? Is being miserable and not able to find joy worth it? I beg to differ.

There even is a second paradox here. We not only work our bums off all the time in the quest towards happiness, but we also dismiss any possibilities of allowing happiness into our lives. In other words, we actually slow down progress and growth, and therefore leave little room to fully enjoy and experience the good in our life. We lose ourselves in our attachment to the goal and forget to reconnect with the present moment. Despite the present being all we ever have. As Eleanor Roosevelt once said: "*Today is a gift. That's why we call it the present*". What if the answer to struggle is "less"? We must fill our own cup until we're overflowing and give from that place instead of scavenging for every last drop to get through another work week.

A quick hack you can try here would be to practise energy management instead of time management. To do this, you must first figure out how much energy a certain task will cost you, and feel into how much energy you currently have. It's also about not working against your natural body clock, if you know you are an early bird, more difficult tasks will be better done in the morning rather than putting in late night sessions. I find this tactic easiest when it comes to physical tasks, like going to the gym or taking the bike to work, but you can absolutely use it for any mental tasks, as that still requires energy. The next step is to check in with yourself and determine whether you have the required energy to get the work done. If you are low on energy, you will need to recharge your batteries first. If you have enough, you can go ahead but might need to recharge after. And no, I don't mean downing another coffee or sipping another energy drink. We are talking about true energy givers like sleep, food, nature, or time with loved ones.

Mini-Exercise: Energy Management

Create a list with all your energy givers and drainers. Also consult the list of activities you have already put together, and check whether you have a balance between the two. If you find you drain yourself more than you recharge, it's a sign for you to schedule in more energy givers.

Believe it or not, watching anime has taught me the magic formula to living a sustainable lifestyle. Particularly the series "Demon Slayer", which is about Tanjiro who becomes a fighter to save his sister who has turned into a demon. (Hang in there, I will get to the point, I promise). Tanjiro's journey can be divided into three different repeating cycles, of which the first one is the rigorous training he undergoes to learn the skills needed to succeed in his mission. He then is immediately challenged to put his learnings into practice whilst facing demons in fights for life or death. These fights take a toll on him so he has to spend some time resting, recharging, and recovering, in order to be able to hone his craft to then face the next challenge. What I deeply love about anime like this one, is how much the main characters continue learning and growing. They never give up, despite how hard the training is or how tough their opponents are. They have a goal, they put in the work and rest, and they achieve it. This way, they are always pushing their boundaries, growing and fine smithing their mindset as well.

Of course, you could argue, "*But Josi, this isn't real.*" But, it actually is very much the same in our reality, too. Life is one, big training session divided up into smaller ones. It's plastered with challenges (the fights) we have to overcome and moments of peace where we get to enjoy the fruit of our labour. We need to rest and recharge before we can charge into the next battle. If anything, the fact that anime characters often seem to rest more compared to us, makes them almost more real, wouldn't you agree?

A Note on Mindfulness

Meditation and mindfulness are two damn powerful ways to take care of yourself. They can also help your mindset. The link between the two is self-awareness. The more aware you are, the better you can work on and shift your mindset. Mindfulness and meditation practices cultivate self-awareness by directing attention to the present moment. They allow you to become more attuned to your thoughts, emotions, and bodily sensations without judgement. This heightened awareness allows you to recognise unhelpful thought patterns, limiting beliefs, and negative emotions, which are all essential aspects of mindset work.

They can also support a positive mindset by encouraging you to focus on positive experiences, gratitude, and (self-)compassion. These practices help you release negative thoughts and emotions, reframe challenges as opportunities for growth, and cultivate a sense of gratitude and optimism. Such positivity and optimism contribute to the development of a growth mindset and the belief that one can always learn and improve.

Lastly, sitting down in peace and quiet can, and will, strengthen your resilience and mental flexibility. Through observing and accepting thoughts and emotions without judgement, you can develop the ability to bounce back from setbacks, adapt to change, and embrace new perspectives. This resilience and mental flexibility are important aspects of mindset work, as they help you overcome challenges and develop a growth-oriented mindset (we will dive into more detail on this specific point later on).

You have already practised and learned some easy ways to tap into mindfulness and meditation. Make it a priority to implement them into your daily routine to reap the best benefits.

Chapter Summary

In this chapter, you learned about the "Resting Paradox" and how crucial it is to recharge if you want to be at the top of your game in a sustainable and most importantly, joyful way. You now have a better understanding of the importance and benefits of mindfulness as one of your self-care practices for a flourishing mindset.

Section Summary

- Through getting crystal clear on your "Why" and setting strong AIM SMART goals, you unlock a deeper motivation within you to make it happen.

- You already have all that you need within, and you can activate any strength that you seek within yourself. You even can turn weaknesses into your secret superpowers. The key to unlocking those strengths is in you deciding to do so, and putting in the action. The more often you do so, the better you will get at it.

- Embodiment is all about energy, how you feel and who you identify as. Whilst many people think that it's all about "having" first so that you can "do" and "be", it is actually the other way around. Through shifting your identity and "being" first you know what to "do" so that you can "have" what you desire.

- A goal without an action is just wishful thinking. Through tapping into your inner resources and asking yourself the questions, "What do you need to do to get where you want to be?" or, "What would my best self do?", you always act from a place of alignment with your higher self. This will inevitably lead to a life of fulfilment and purpose.

- Self-care is the secret productivity hack that will make the journey towards achieving your goals and becoming the leader of your life more enjoyable and sustainable.

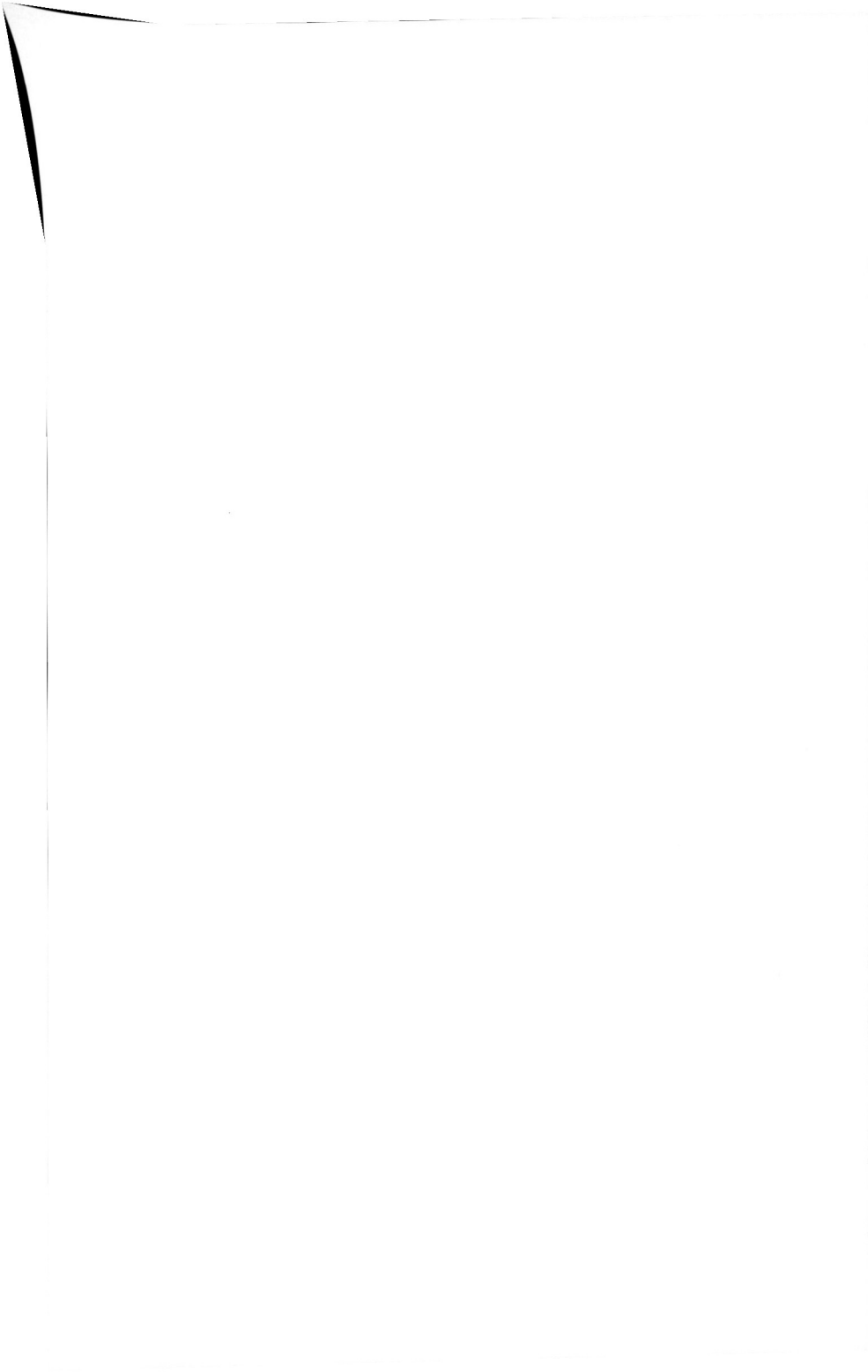

Section 4:
The Journey

Chapter 11: Living a Life of Purpose

Move with purpose, be with intention.

Well, my dear, we have reached the point where you have the foundation and the necessary tools to embark on this journey. I mean, yeah, you could already count all of the work until now as a part of the journey. But in this section, we will focus on what keeps you going. You will learn how to navigate and work around challenges that you must face along the way. you will learn additional tips and tricks to help you go from novice to master in your mind and ultimately. turn into a real leader of your own life.

After all, life is a journey. And every person is on their very own journey. Some might cross in a supportive or less supportive way, but it's nevertheless a lesson for you to learn. Some people may be in each other's lives for longer, while others may leave too early. With some, you might be connected through blood yet don't want them to be part of your life for valid reasons. Others you may be connected to through friendship or experiences, and you have the closest bond there is. Some people you might admire but you never actually meet, or sometimes you think that you know someone only to then learn you didn't know them at all. The point I'm getting to is: other humans come and go throughout your life. The only relationship you never will lose is the one to yourself.

Because we are pack animals, we seek connection. Yet, the most important connection is the one that we have with ourselves. Establishing this bond, understanding how we tick, listening to our intuition and our instincts, and more importantly, following what we feel called to do, is why we are truly here. Our soul purpose is hugely different from reproduction and survival. Finding it, and making it real... *that's* the journey. That's the key to living a life without regret, a life of purpose and a life you *love*. And some life purposes might look bigger than others, but that doesn't matter. The fulfilment and joy that comes through living it is for every person the same. I once heard a story about a lady who absolutely loves kids and making their trip to school fun and exciting. Everyday, she greets them with the biggest smile, she knows their names and looks after them in her own, unique way. She is living her purpose. Others may want to create a huge movement that impacts thousands of lives. But at the core, they both are the same.

Each person is making this world a better place through living their purpose their way. Therefore, don't ever compare yours to someone else's.

Maybe until now, you haven't lived your purpose, or maybe you even loathed your life. But it's never too late. In fact, there's no such thing as late, because time is simply a continuous moment of *now*. What you ever truly experience is now. Whatever happened in the past is now non-existent, staying alive only due to mere memories. Whatever you think is in the future doesn't exist at all; it's just your perception and expectation of what is. The perfect moment to do something, to start leading your life the way you want, is *now*. And the main tool you will ever need in your toolkit is: Don't give up, keep going. You already do that anyway. Regardless of the challenges life has thrown at you thus far, no matter how far "back" it may have pushed you, you are still here because you kept going. This is the power of this ultimate ally that you have: your best self.

You find on this journey that it is always *you* who got you to where you are. Perhaps you had support or good connections, but you made the final call. That decision that changed everything. The same methods that got you to where you are now are what will get you to where you want to be: one step at a time. The only difference is the direction you choose to go. So, if you can go anywhere anyway, and you are already doing that, why not go somewhere where you like what you see from your window seat?

This is why I would never turn back and give up my dream of becoming a worldwide-known and sought-after coach. I love the view and I love the destination. But, for a while, I also loved the idea of becoming a CFO. There's no denying that it was a dream of mine. But it changed, and that's okay. Dreams, like opinions are allowed to change. Another example would be that for a long time, I didn't want to have kids, then I met my boyfriend and it all changed. He literally got my ovaries singing, something I never experienced before. What should not change when it comes to your goals, is the fact that you keep pursuing them. Regret only ever happens when you do things that you were never aligned with, or because your saboteurs were in control, and you feared what others might think, that they would abandon you, or judge you.

The beauty of this is, they will judge you no matter what. Whether you are living your dream life or not, those who have not established their own bond with their true selves and have given full control to their saboteurs will judge you. If you are being judged anyway, why not do the thing that you love most? Why not lead by example, heal yourself, make cool shit happen and show others that if you can do it, so can they? If I would have given any shit about the judgement I faced along the way, you wouldn't be reading this book right now. People threw things at me like: "*You are too young to be a coach*", "*You are too late to start your own business*", "*You will never make it in Finance*", "*You have nothing to write about, no one will read your stuff*", "*Self-employment is not safe, get a proper job*", etc. The thing about each of these statements is that they're excuses for the people who phrased them, *not* to implement a change in their own lives. It's a common saboteur reaction to ward off what could cause a change to the norm (saboteurs *love* the norm and hate new or different). Imagine that if all of these people were to stop immediately judging and avoiding what's different (hello, fixed mindset), and instead, they embrace it (hello, growth mindset)? Imagine them embracing their personality, doing their own thing, and loving it.

They are starting the side hustle at the age of forty, writing a book about their heartbreak so that they can heal at the age of twenty-five, and are following their passion and purpose when they turn seventy. They would be a hell of a lot happier. Just saying.

Don't ever let someone else's judgement stop you from living your best life.

One beautiful aspect of integrity and diversity is to embrace change in others and oneself, and to not fight one's truth, nor dismiss someone else's due to ones own insecurities. Imagine the cascade effect that your actions can have on others if you decide to live your life and let others live theirs. People will see you and feel inspired to chase their own dreams. Imagine how different the world would be if everyone realised their own power, followed their dreams, and gave zero shit about having to stop others from pursuing theirs because they aren't afraid of their own potential any more. Give this thought a second to incubate. Whenever I think about this, it gives me the chills. And it reconfirms why I do what I do. Knowing how crazy capable you are and understanding that you are worthy of pursuing your dreams, that you have all that you need to become the CEO of your one and only role: life. This is my journey, my mission, and my big vision.

For your journey, what is your big vision and/or your big agenda? In other words, what is your Grammy moment? How will you, when you lead by example, change this world? What is it that you will make real in this world? What is your soul purpose?

At the beginning of this book, we decided on a single goal of how you want to uplift your life to a ten. This question relates to how you will make the experience on this planet a ten. But your purpose goes a step further, and this next exercise will help you to phrase it.

Exercise: Your Billboard

Close your eyes and ground yourself in the natural rhythm of your breathing. In your mind's eye, imagine the biggest billboard you have ever seen. Every human on this planet will pass this billboard. What will you put on it? What do you want every other human in this world to see? What message will you convey? What pictures might be on it? What colours are you using? Are any word highlighted? How will this message transform yourself and others? See it in front of you with all its details. When you are ready, open your eyes again and feel free to even draw that billboard onto a piece of paper.

To capture the essence of this exercise, you can use this prompt to decide on your very own soul purpose, mission, or vision:

"I am the (metaphor/who you are) that (impact/ what you are contributing to this world.)"

Here's an example of my first ever draft of this statement: *"I am the genie who lights up people to live their wildest dreams and unlocks their highest potential."* Or here is a beautiful example of one of my clients: *"I am owning and leaning into my feminine leadership, sailing beyond horizons to connect and make a big impact."*

And today, my love, is day one of living your life of your purpose. You may find that as you go on this journey, your statement, or even your purpose, will slightly change. There is no rule that says you can only have one purpose, or that it is set in stone once you have nailed one down. As you grow and change, your purpose will grow and change. The same goes for the challenges you will face, the allies you will need, and the people in your life. You might even find that you will get to live your purpose in a completely different way than you imagined at first. Most of the time, it's even better.

Honesty Hour

As I want you to be fully prepared for this journey, and not sugar-coat the reality of levelling up, I do want to shed some light on the cost of doing so. This is why some people might never even try to pursue what they actually want to do and instead choose the pain or cost of regret. However, the cost of levelling up pales in comparison to the alternative cost of regret for not pursuing our dreams and aspirations. And even more importantly, you are not "some people", otherwise you wouldn't be reading this book. But, what does it take when deciding to have faith and make the empowered choice to pursue a fulfilling life on purpose?

You have to embrace uncertainty and be willing to step into the unknown.

There is no blueprint you can follow; you are the one who must create your own roadmap to your success. However, this also means that with every step you take, you will discover new strengths, unlock hidden potential, and cultivate resilience. You learn to figure stuff out and learn by doing so along the way. (Prime example from my side: since starting my own business I learned to master more than thirteen systems to set everything up in the back-end of my business. This also made me appreciate it so much more when looking at other websites or processes, as I know how much time and work goes into all of it).

You need to be dedicated to your goals and disciplined enough to show up every day to take the required and most importantly consistent action.

You will need to invest time and energy (as you would with staying where you are). The difference is the journey, because you know that you do it for yourself and your own happiness. This feeling is irreplaceable. The rewards gained in terms of personal satisfaction and growth far outweigh the investment. Staying where you are now is a choice, too, and requires discipline as well. So, why not invest that energy into your dreams and give them a shot?

You will feel discomfort on a daily basis as you keep on pushing beyond your comfort zone.

You will face fears and take risks. But, this is also what will expand your limits, crush your self-doubt, develop new perspectives, and become a leader in life and inspiration for others. You are embodying paving a path of self-belief and opportunities, and this is what will change the world. Staying in the hamster wheel and conforming to all the norms and expectations may grant you an easy life but will not create the change you want to see in this world. It takes you to do it. No one else.

Whilst these may be valid worries, choosing to forego personal growth is settling for a life of comfort and mediocrity because it may seem easier in the short term. Yes, I said it, and do you know why? Because you are *so* worthy and capable of so much more!!! Not only that, the cost of regret can be significant and long-lasting. Regret arises from the realisation that you never pursued your dreams or fully embraced your potential. It can lead to feelings of stagnation, unfulfilled potential, and a life tinged with "what if's." As Gary Vaynerchuk describes it in his book "*Twelve and a Half*", "*Regret is the biggest poison of them all,*" and that when we need to use conviction, ambition and tenacity to push our limits and take the leap. In fact, confidence is merely a by-product of conviction. If you are convinced you will reach your goal, no matter what, and you keep on stepping outside the zone of self-limitation (a.k.a. your comfort zone) you will inevitably grow your confidence in the process. Believe you can, and confidence will follow.

To live a life completely free of regret, always remember this one question: What do you want to remember the most about yourself and your life when looking back at old age?

Choosing to give your best life a chance will never lead to regret. Only burying your dreams will. Choosing to grow will never, ever make your life worse off than it is now; it can only improve! The Return of Investment is exactly what you put in and is utterly in your control. Knowing this, why would you not do it?

Chapter Summary

Despite being short and sweet, this chapter led you to find your purpose or mission statement that will accompany you from now on, and will be the North Star of your journey. You now have all of the tools you need to take one step at a time, and you know that you can trust yourself to have the impact on others that you seek. You are ready to live a life free of regret. You are ready to live a life you love. You are ready for making your dream become reality and live your life on purpose.

Chapter 12: When Shit Hits the Fan

Life's a roller-coaster, enjoy the ride.

I already touched on the cost of levelling up briefly in the previous chapter. As you go on this journey of living your best and most fulfilled life, you will face new challenges, new hurdles, and new *"What the actual fucks?!"* There will be moments when you might think that you are back to ground zero or things are plateauing. This is not to discourage you; this is to help you be fully prepared for when shit hits the fan. Therefore, you know how to deal with setbacks in the form of self-doubt, or any other typical self-sabotaging behaviours.

The one thing that will get you through any challenge is resilience. I will tell you right here and now that you already have a hell of a lot of resilience because otherwise, you wouldn't be reading this book in the first place. So far, you have faced and survived all of the big and small challenges that life has thrown at you, which means that there is no doubt you will also be able to face any new ones coming your way. I'm pointing this out to nip the self-doubt that might be creeping up in the butt. But, I also want to show you different ways in which you can further train your resilience. Yes, it can be trained, as can mostly anything!

The best way to go about it is through creating your own blueprint of life when attempting the seemingly impossible.

People have told me that it's impossible to make it as a coach, or to build and run your own business. Today, it's two years later and there is no end in sight at all. On the contrary, we are just getting started and bigger things will be coming. More life-changing impact is to be made, and more women like you are to be supported in their journey. Yes, it's hard at times. Yes, there's doubt at times, but it is the tools and the constant mindset work that keeps me going, believing, and making awesome shit happen. To follow your purpose means to become your own trailblazer (hello again, jungle-path metaphor!) You must map out the path that no one has walked before, because no one can actually walk it except for you. Others are walking their paths, and they might cross, or you might support one another, but the path you are on is just for you. And it is in your responsibility to create your very own blueprint. However, the one and most important thing is to believe that it *is* possible for you to do that.

To support you in this, strengthen your mindset, and build your resilience even further, we will dive into some lessons originating from stoicism. Though I always think that's just another label for tools to get you further in life. But, let's go with it for a moment. First up, what exactly is stoicism and why does it gain more and more popularity nowadays?

Stoicism is an ancient Greek philosophy that has gained renewed interest in recent years due to its practical applications in modern life, including in leadership roles. At its core, stoicism is about cultivating inner resilience and equanimity in the face of adversity, and focusing on what is within our control, rather than getting bogged down by external factors. It offers a practical and powerful framework to assist in making grounded decisions, maintain composure in stressful situations, focus on your own actions rather than trying to control others, inspire your team with a shared sense of purpose, and create a positive, productive work (life) environment.

As you are creating your own blueprint and dealing with the setbacks and challenges along the way, you are already building resilience. It is seeing setbacks and failures not as permanent stumbling blocks, but rather stepping stones towards success. It is in the act of stopping to play the victim player role and get yourself out of the shithole. Instead of dwelling on disappointment, learn from your mistakes, adapt quickly, and bounce back stronger than before. This will empower you to face challenges head-on, persevere through adversity, and maintain that unwavering determination. For example, when I was burnt out, depressed and found myself in a toxic relationship and work environment, I could have called it quits. But I didn't. Instead, I decided that I will not be the victim of this story, but become the woman who rose from the ashes and turned her life around. And I did. And so can you. It is in your power and choice to become more resilient. Another way to increase your resilience is through putting yourself in situations where you are most likely to experience failure. These situations may include learning new skills or taking on a new hobby. Do something that you have never done before, and you will experience the teaching nature of the beginner's mind. To get the most out of it and progress quickly, go by the concept of failing fast, so you can learn, and try again. The key here is to continue trying and trying because it is only those who persevere through the discomfort of failing who will reap true success. If you give into the little nagging voice that says, "*If you stop, you will feel better,*" you have lost the stoic challenge and missed a chance in growing your self-trust. By consciously putting yourself out there and facing these struggles in the zone of discomfort, you step into a heroic role in life and transform your being, as you come back stronger and more resilient from each challenge.

However, when you face a challenge, like being stuck in traffic, or the water hose in the house breaks, there are actually two setback challenges that you must overcome. William B. Irvine describes it brilliantly in his book "*The Stoic Challenge*". He calls it the "*post-setback setback challenge*". This challenge comes with the emotional reaction to the first setback. If you let yourself go down the rabbit hole of frustration and anger, you will experience a setback in terms of emotional and mental exhaustion as you lose control over the rush of negative emotions and let yourself be crushed by their weight. Please note that I'm exaggerating these reactions and examples. This being said, it all comes down to the same principle. Allowing negative emotions (or saboteurs) to take over your life, in any way, will not lead to happiness. You've already learned that negative feelings won't get you anywhere. Or even worse, you may "infect" someone else with your negative attitude. Yes, of course, you want to be understood.

Yes of course, you may have all the reasons to be angry. Yes, of course, it's not wise to swallow your emotions and hide them away until you explode. However, do negative emotions really lead to positive progress? No. Can you make clear-headed decisions that are aligned with your values when you are swarmed by negative feelings? No. Do you really want to carry your negative memories all the way up into old age? No. Use the tools from chapters three and four to turn the challenge on its head, and create something positive from it.

Exercise: Bring It On!

A fun way to do exactly this is through gamifying when you are dealing with hardships. The idea is simple: the next time you face a setback, make it a test of your resilience and resourcefulness and *choose* to go at it full power. Say to yourself,"*Oh you want to test me? Come right at me, I'm ready!!!*" Doing this may shift your attitude towards the hardship and you will feel more resilient taking it on. Or, you can just ask yourself, "*What about this change is making me happy?*". This will sway your focus back to the positives of this situation and will help you feel better about it all. You can then celebrate yet another triumph of building more resilience. I know it may sound contradictory at first, but give it a try and see what comes up for you.

A client of mine once came into the session just after a chain reaction of setbacks. She was furious and bogged down by several events that happened the day before. It started with the plane being delayed, the suitcase taking ages, getting stuck in traffic, and went on to being extremely tired and coming late into a call with a client. You name it, it was a shitty day and she felt frustrated about it. After giving her a couple minutes to just vent, voice, and acknowledge her experience, I asked her, "*What are you thrilled about that this has happened?*" This question interrupted her self-sabotaging thought spiral and she realised that there were many things to be grateful for in all this. For example, she was thrilled that she could get on a call with a dear friend and that she got some extra time to get some work done. And it's easy to overlook those moments of goodness in our lives when we are in the midst of a shitstorm. But that makes it even more important to look for them and not let one unfortunate event ruin your whole day. When I look back at the time of being burnt out, all I can think now is, "*thank goodness!*" Because it made me realise what was really going on, how misaligned I was with what I wanted, and that I deserved to feel a lot happier. And it was the curtain drop I needed to change my life.

Many people who have experienced incredible hardship or have had to endure horrific things and unfairness, managed to turn their lives around through focusing on the lessons they learned and to use that knowledge to create more good in this world. This doesn't mean that they don't express sadness, anger, or frustration, but rather to express those feelings and then move on with the lessons. I know not always everyone manages to do so, but dare I say this is due to choice. If you stay stuck in self-pity, then you are in the self-sabotage mode of the victim player, and no positive change will ever come from that.

These are the moments when you've got to step into your power, and take ownership, even if the shit that hit your fan was unfair or not supposed to happen.

I sometimes call these challenges or periods being in the "phoenix era" because everything seems to be burning to the ground. But at the same time, it makes space for you to be completely reborn from the ashes. The universe sometimes likes doing funny things like this, especially if you have been stuck for too long, but in the end it's always in your favour.

The tactics we discussed until now were mainly focused on external challenges and how to deal with them according to the rules of stoicism. But, what about the challenges that originate from within? We already looked thoroughly at how we might be self-sabotaging and playing small due to our upbringing and programming. The following three challenges that we will look at originate from the same space. I have found that most of my clients endure these challenges throughout their journey. Imposter Syndrome (which really is just a fancy word for saying self-doubt), procrastination, and being stuck in the same (most of the time negative) perspective, are what threaten to hold them back most.

How To Overcome Imposter Syndrome & Self-Doubt

Imposter Syndrome can be described as the fear of being called out as a fraud. Those who struggle with it, fail to believe that they are actually good at what they do. It's a form of self-doubt that can cause anxiety, depression, and lead to burnout. Imposter Syndrome is a collection of different behaviour patterns that include perfectionism (setting unattainable standards and never feeling capable enough), heroism (needing to be the best), and fear of failure (feeling shame and guilt if they cannot meet expectations). In simpler words, Imposter Syndrome occurs when you find arguments against yourself and your own capabilities, making you feel powerless and pulverising your self-trust. (Does it ring a bell? Hello Victim-Player!) Doubt and worry only exist because you choose to attach meaning to the beliefs that you aren't good enough.

As with the change of any behaviour pattern, this cannot just be fixed overnight. It always comes back to the continuous practice and choice of shifting your belief and behaviour system over time. Experiencing setbacks along the way are totally normal and to be expected. The key is to rinse and repeat this process as often as needed to retrain your brain and create new behaviour and thought patterns.

Step 1:

Become extra aware of when you are experiencing the fear of being called out or feeling not good enough or valuable enough. The more awareness you have, the more opportunities you will find to practise a new experience. You may want to do this pre-emptively before a specific event when you know that the Imposter Saboteur might pop up. If you catch yourself in the moment, don't forget to first disrupt your current thought pattern with a breathing technique. This way, you can mentally take a step back and observe the situation with more clarity. Or you do it after the fact as a reflection exercise.

Step 2:

Name all of the emotions that you are experiencing like anger, frustration, or shame (use The Emotions Wheel if you need help) and write out the exact thoughts that you are having. For example: "*I shouldn't be this successful, I don't know shit!*", "*I feel like I'm just winging it*", or "*I feel like I'm missing out, all others seem to know a secret that I don't know!*" Then, ask yourself whether all of these thoughts are really true and helpful to you. Maybe there are certain skills you truly need to master in order to not feel like an amateur or imposter, but as I have experienced with most of my clients, they do have the experience but don't dare to own it or count upon it.

Step 3:

Release these thoughts and beliefs, with the process you learned in chapter three. Feel free to burn the piece of paper or rip it into pieces to really emphasise that they no longer hold power over you. Take a new piece of paper and write new beliefs to replace them. This could look like: "*I know I am* capable and smart, I deserve to be here, and I trust myself." Take it a step further and list a minimum of ten things that you are grateful for achieving to refuel your confidence and self-belief. Remind yourself of what challenges you have already overcome, or when you stood up for yourself will also remind you that you can indeed do hard things. You are your own best proof, and you already have come far, be proud.

Step 4:

Set your intention of how you want to live, and be with this new thought and behaviour pattern. You might even want to consult your best self or remind yourself of your values, and use them as your inner compass. As you move ahead, create an accomplishment list, and on a daily basis collect proof that you are incredibly smart and capable of doing what you do. Celebrate your wins, learn from setbacks, share your experience, and be kind to yourself.

Step 5:

Repeat these steps whenever you notice the old thoughts popping up. It can also be in your imagination. It's a continuous cycle of recognising, releasing, re-framing, and recreating. It might not ever fully disappear, but know that it's normal. As you grow and evolve, so will your circumstances and challenges. Luckily, you now have all the tools to overcome them all.

As a rule of thumb, you can also apply this simple trick: Whatever thought of self-doubt comes up, debunk it by re-affirming the opposite and remind yourself with proof why the doubtful thought isn't true. If you are thinking, "*I'm not good enough*", turn it into, "*I am good enough!*"

Overcoming Procrastination

This fact about procrastination might surprise you, but hopefully it also completely shifts how you see it. (I'm aiming for an upcoming aha-moment here!) Procrastination is just a stress-response. Aha! If I'm less stressed, I will procrastinate less. You got it, dear!

In general, procrastination is known as the art of pushing out specific tasks until the last minute or even dropping them completely. It is a gap between your intention of doing something and the actual action. You already know the self-sabotage type, the Excuse-Finder, which represents this form of playing small. It might not come as a surprise to you, but in fact any self-sabotaging type could be seen as procrastination. The Perfectionist spends too much time getting the picture frame exactly even, the Overdoer' continues doing irrelevant tasks, the Overthinker ruminates on past events for way too long, and the "Analyser" can't make up her mind. In this next part, however, I want to go into a little bit more detail so that you can truly understand procrastination fully and stop it in its tracks.

From a pure psychological point of view, there are mainly two different forms of procrastination. Both of them are stress responses from the body, meaning that your brain in this moment perceives a threat and gets into fight, flight, or freeze mode. It's a survival response to the threat in the form of stress that you are experiencing, even if it is only subtle. You might even say, *"But I feel fine, how come I'm stressed?!"* This is where it is helpful to go inwards and backwards for a moment. What are you truly feeling right now? What is your heart rate like? Do you experience racing thoughts? What happened throughout your day. Was it actually more stressful than you thought? Or, has something triggered a traumatic response? Has a saboteur within you made you feel more overwhelmed than usual? How were your last couple of weeks or months? Did your work increase? Did you have to deal with a tricky project? Answering these questions will provide some insight as to what caused the stress in your external and internal environment, your thought patterns, and your self-talk. They will also help you understand which circumstances might be causing which form of procrastination.

One of which is productive procrastination. This type of behaviour makes you think that you are doing something that is of service to you, but in fact: it's not. Have you ever wondered why you might have a sudden urge to clean your entire house when you initially planned to update your CV? Or did you ever catch yourself reading up on a subject for months and months, telling yourself that you need to learn more first? Or did you turn into an expert planner, mapping out every five minutes of your new daily routine starting next week, only to find yourself struggling with the allocated times and needing to reschedule everything and staying in planning mode versus execution mode? This type of procrastination tricks you into thinking that you actually accomplished something, but when it comes down to the real needle-moving activities that will get you closer to achieving your goals (like writing that CV), you have done exactly zero work. (Okay, maybe you wrote one line, then the dishwasher peeped and your saboteur immediately welcomed the distraction, and you ended up doing everything on your to-do list except for that one thing you intended to.)

When you are experiencing this form of procrastination, then you have an overflow of energy. So to get out of the fight-or-flight mode, try releasing some of it in a different and controlled form or to get yourself calm and grounded again. This might be doing a couple of jumping jacks, a short walk around the block followed by breathing exercises, a mini-meditation, or gazing at the passing clouds for a while. This will get you back into a grounded state so that you can make clear decisions and rid your system of this franticness.

The other form of procrastination is caused by the freeze response of your body. In this state, your body shuts down and you may find yourself not wanting to move at all, incredibly tired, and only capable of scrolling through TikTok or binge-watching "The Office" for the third time. You might have guessed that, if you needed to down-regulate in the fight-or-flight mode, you now need to up-regulate your nervous system. Physical activity, again, is the number one antidote to do so, but slowly. If you have been turning into a couch potato, stand up, walk around, and gently stretch your body before you do burpees or dance to your favourite song. You can also try out different breathwork techniques like pranayama, which is often practised in yoga to increase oxygen supply and reduce any toxins in your body. One of my go-tos is a very fast breathing method, in which you sit upright and breathe in very fast through your nose, in and out, without fully filling your lungs. Count up to 50 breaths and then observe its effect on your body for a moment. I personally always experience a tingle in my chest, and I feel more energised after.

If that's not enough to pull yourself out of the excuse-finder mode, follow the exercises I shared with you in chapter three. Acknowledge that you have been procrastinating and forgive yourself for doing so. Then consult your best self to decipher what would be the next best step to get out of it, then do that and get the ball rolling again. Remember that, even if you have been an expert-procrastinator until now, you get to decide whether or not you continue to have this be part of your identity.

You get to choose if, from now on, you are the person who gets herself out of it and continues on.

Return to the "Why" you set out on this journey and remind yourself of the cost you must pay if you continue putting off updating your CV versus working on it for a little bit every day so you can apply for that role that's just made for you and that you know will make you happy. This is also where you practise discernment and see the procrastination for what it really is: a stress response followed by short-term pleasure as a solution because it makes you feel good now. This will provide you with the insight and clarity to get into counteraction.

When Stuck In The Same Perspective

A key element of coaching entails the art of shifting perspectives. Whilst it might sound easy, it is surprising how many people just do *not* do it when they feel stuck in a certain problem or challenge. All they focus on is that it doesn't work, it's too hard, it sucks, and there is no other way. I often even have clients tell me, "*I already explored all of the options there are.*" My answer always is, "*Well, let's explore some more.*" These two practices that I want to share with you have never failed to completely open up the realm to what's possible for my clients. Before we dive into the first method, I want to share with you a short success story, where it took one session and a simple shift in perspective, and my client Sam felt ready to take a big leap and move abroad.

When Sam came to me, she had the big dream of moving abroad with her family. She wanted to see new shores and go on a new adventure. But despite her strong desire to make this happen, she also got stuck in worries about the finances. She thought to herself, "*What if it doesn't work out, and we lose it all and have to come back?*"

Yup, her mind was full stuck in the worst-case scenario. Several saboteurs were running the show for her. There was the Critic, who also feared what others would think if it wouldn't work out (specifically family members who raised concern). Then the "Analyser" and Overthinker, who kept on ruminating and thinking about the same problems and stressors of having to move and invest money, over and over again, without ever getting to a conclusion. They kept her stuck in a lack mentality.

We worked through the saboteurs, gave them a moment to raise their concerns, then simply sent them out of the room so that Sam could instead ask her best self for guidance. This provided Sam the clarity she needed to realise how she was holding herself back from following her dreams, and also reminded her that she can trust herself to work things out, as she has always done. However, she was still not at a place where she felt confident enough to commit and we focused on exploring different perspectives. Up until then, she always looked at her dream from the angle of lack, worry, high risk, and cost. As mentioned, the question, *"What if it goes wrong and we lose everything?"* was her dominant thought.

I asked Sam, "E*ven if you were to lose everything, what would you still gain?"* This question allowed her to accept that taking this risk would be not only a financial matter, but also an investment in herself, her family would learn and grow along the way and experience living in the country they dreamed to live in for so long. You should have seen the look on her eyes as she realised, that she would always win if she would choose so. The money wouldn't be lost because she would be richer in memories and feelings of happiness. That same day, Sam told her partner that she was ready to take the leap. A couple of months later, she had booked a one-way ticket for the entire family. Now, she's living her dream life in her dream country, working in her dream job, and living life to the max. Without financial struggles.

In this example, we simply turned the perspective around, switching it from, "*What if it goes wrong?*" to "*What would still go right?*" If you pair that with debunking the old, limiting belief, a lot more is possible again. Sometimes, it is even enough to ask, "*What would be the absolute worst case scenario, and how likely is it really?*" This allows the brain to make peace with the worst that could happen, as most often than not, it's not very likely to happen if it were to occur. Another way to shift the perspective would be to think about how one's worst case scenario would still be someone else's best case scenario. Many people dream of living comfortably in the UK or having a corporate job. Reminding oneself of that never fails to ease the anxiety around that possibility.

Other similar methods that do the same thing are to zoom in and out of the challenge. We already practised this a little bit with the questions, "*If you don't change anything, what will life continue to look like in one, five, ten, or thirty years from now?*" , "*Imagine you are on your deathbed, what would you want to have chosen to do?*" or, "*What do you want to be remembered for?*" Zooming out means that you look at the current situation from the perspective of an X amount of years down the line. Or, you could use a metaphor and look at everything from the top of the mountain so that you can see what happened before, and what might happen after. This helps to take off the blinders and see the full picture again. Most of the time, my clients then learn that the problem they face right now is not even that relevant. Or, they look at it from the viewpoint of their kids and decide how they want to lead as an example for them. This way, they find a completely new approach to solve it. In addition, this process interrupts the saboteur's way of thinking, and instead, you get the chance to take a step back and choose which way to go.

One of the most exciting ways to switch up your perspective is through taking random objects, places, colours, people, your allies, or a complete mix of any of them, to find new ways of looking at the issue. In one session, I offered my client the perspective of the pineapple as we were talking about her next steps in her career. I simply grabbed this golden and pearly coloured candy jar that looks like a pineapple and straight up asked her, *"What comes up for you when looking at this pineapple?"* I kid you not, as random as this might sound, my client resonated so much with what she was discovering in the pineapple perspective (like ease and joy), that it ended up being her chosen perspective. From that day on, the pineapple was a symbol that she carried with her even after to continue reminding herself of the meaning. In other sessions with different clients various objects or even animals like paintings, empty bottles, aeroplanes, pillows, or dogs were leading to incredible insight and advice. The reason is that when you change the way you look at things, the things you look at change. That's when you then get to make an empowered decision that will help you to turn the shit that hit the fan into gold. The thing is, when you look at a situation through the lens of pessimism, you will always find a problem.

If you look at everything through optimism, paired with kindness to yourself, you won't make one wrong decision.

Chapter Summary

In this chapter, we pre-tackled common challenges like self-doubt and procrastination that you most likely will face along this journey. Life happens, and you won't be able to completely control it, but what you *can* control is how you receive what life throws at you. Remember: it is your choice whether life happens to or for you, and resilience is always going for the latter. The journey is supposed to be a roller-coaster of highs and lows, and there is goodness to be found in both. This is true whether it's a lesson to be learned, or just enjoying riding on high waves.

Chapter 13: Commitment to Your Best Self

*The most important promises you make
are the ones to yourself.*

The examples of the transformations that you have read in this book are here so that you can see exactly what is possible for you when you start shifting your mindset and put in the work towards your goals. We often think that we are the only ones who struggle with burnout, negative self-talk, procrastination, imposter syndrome, and more. Especially now that we spend even more time in our own four walls and less in actual companionship with others. This leads to a tunnel vision that can cause us to feel lonely and misunderstood. If this is paired with being hijacked by saboteurs, it is even more difficult to collect the proof of your magnificence and capability. I hope that this book has taught you the ins and outs of what it takes to work yourself through that low, realise your potential, and overcome any challenges or limits you endure.

In the last chapter, you began creating a list of accomplishments. This is also a list of proof that you absolutely can do the things you long for. The desires that you have are there for a reason. They are there because you are meant to follow them. And they can be so uniquely different from person to person, but they all stem from this deep wish of creating something meaningful in this life that we have. The only true lesson we need to learn is to follow this calling. For some, this might be entrepreneurship. For others, it is climbing the corporate ladder. Some may want to be the best mum ever. Others long to travel and tell stories of the world. Or, it might even be a combination of all three. Heck, it could even be that it changes throughout your life and that is okay, too. Whatever it is that your dream is, go after it, give it a try, and make some awesome shit happen.

I want to point out that if someone else did it, then it doesn't take anything away from your ability to do it.

On the contrary, the fact that you know that it is possible for someone else, is another proof to be added to your list that you can do it, too. You notice other people acing at their life because you were always meant to do the same. As you shift your mindset with all the exercises in this book, you will learn to look at this world and others from a place of abundance rather than a place of lack. Simply because someone else got a slice of a cake, it doesn't mean that you can't have one. The cake is infinite, and you choose which one you have and how much of it. So, take all of the examples of incredible transformations in this book as signs that you will be the next to accomplish great things.

With this, my dear, it is now time to take a step towards your new reality. You have set a SMART goal, you know the minimum viable product that you want to achieve, and you know exactly why you want to achieve it and how it will change your life. You've also learned tips and tricks as to how you can hold yourself accountable when we explored habits and actions. You know how your saboteurs might try to hold you back and continue watching from the side-lines. But, you also know your strengths and how to turn any perceived weakness into another strength to help you overcome your self-imposed limits. You know how to deal with life when shit hits the fan. You have proof that incredible change is possible for you too. So, what's left?

Committing to yourself

This form of commitment seems to be one of the hardest, for some almost impossible, despite their big dreams and hopes begging them to chase after them. Astonishingly, this also seems to be a lot easier to drop than when it comes to commitment to others. When it comes to actually committing to action and working towards it, people sometimes freeze up and stop. Most of the time, the reason is because their saboteurs want to try everything to keep them from the experience of failure. Any excuse is a welcome loophole that could provide a way out. But giving in to one's excuses is not what creates momentum and also not what makes amazing shit happen in this world.

And I get it. This is due to caring a lot more about what others think of us than we do (even if you don't want to admit it). It is not unusual for humans to put more emphasis on others' opinions. They seek out advice, want to be accepted, and yearn to belong to the group. They do a lot in order to please others' expectations of them. It's partially due to human nature, yet in the instances of living the life you desire to live, this can be of high disservice. It also is a deep-rooted, societal issue where you get trained to follow a certain lifestyle, plan, or journey. But, this takes away the autonomy to follow your own path and what you are meant to do, as well as your authority in being yourself.

Self-leadership means that you reclaim that autonomy. It means that you claim your right of leadership over your life back. It means stepping out of the victim mentality, overthinking, self-doubt, procrastinating, and working your ass off for others and not yourself.

It's about going your way, despite all the odds,
to find your way to make it work.

Working on yourself and fully committing to yourself allows you to go through a gradual metamorphosis. You'll begin to perceive yourself as the driving force behind your own journey, capable of making mindful choices, and leading yourself towards your goals. Armed with a newfound confidence and clarity, you'll step into self-leadership, embracing the role of the author who is shaping your life's narrative the way you want. Let's create a waterproof contract with yourself, free from loopholes. Dropping out of the commitment to yourself from now on, simply is not even an option any more

Exercise: Create Your Commitment Statement

Bring it all together into words and onto paper, create a contract or a promise with yourself about what you are going to make real in this world. And I dare you to not skip this step or to let your saboteurs build in some sneaky traps that give you a way out. This is when you must practise determination, and most importantly, keep on practising it as you go. If there is any doubt left at this point, reframe your perspective of commitment. If until now you have often found yourself breaking your promises to yourself, or not being able to stick to new habits, or being stern with breaking the old ones, return to chapter three and work through the process to shift that limiting belief that currently persists around commitment. Just because things have been this way in the past, there is zero evidence that you can't do it now. The past can't be changed, so all the evidence you need to make it happen lies in your future. What is your best self's perspective on commitment? I bet you that she knows she's got this. She trusts herself and she knows that she can do hard things.

Here is my current perspective of commitment that I designed with my best self in mind: "*My perspective to commitment is to walk the talk of inspired actions towards my purpose and using my heart as my compass.*" This statement is actually taped to my wall right next to me, so I see it every day. It reminds me to refuse to do life any other way, because for me personally, I know that this is what leads me to the greatest fulfilment and alignment with my highest self.

Take a moment to write down your perspective of commitment, as it probably was until now, and then write another version of how it will be from now on. In addition, write down what you are saying "Yes" to, starting today, as well as what you are saying "No" to.

Here's what this might look like (from the same sticky note on my wall):

- *"I say "Yes" to: just doing it."*
- *"I say "Yes" to: being a confident trailblazer."*
- *"I say "Yes" to: honouring my values"*
- *"I say "No" to: overthinking and overcomplicating"*
- *"I say "No" to: self-doubt"*
- *"I say "No" to: my saboteurs"*

What do you need to say "Yes" and "no" to in order to make your dreams become reality, become the leader of your life, and take ownership of who you are? Check in with yourself and decide whether saying "Yes" to this action feels expansive and intuitive, or dreadful, contractive, and heavy. If it's the latter, rethink whether it really is what you need to do, or whether you are coming from a place of fear and not intuition. Fear is never a bad thing, and there is no need to "devilise" it. Instead, be curious about it and decide whether it is a legitimate warning because you truly are in danger, or because you are about to venture into the unknown. The latter is where you take fear by its hand and say, *"Let's explore together!"*

Now that this is cleared, we can work on your actual commitment statement. Here is a template that you can use, but feel free to adapt and change as needed to make it work for you. You might even want to write several statements and develop a new one for every week, including your main goal for the week and what you will do to achieve it and hold yourself accountable. The possibilities for this are endless, and as long as it resonates with you and excites you, that's all that matters.

Commitment Statement Template:

As of today [current date], I [Your Full Name], am making the commitment to myself to [what you are committing to]. I declare that I will take the appropriate steps forward with my focus and dedication to activate [the version/identity of you, that you're becoming]. The steps that I will take are the following:

[list out each action you will take from now on, including how often and when. Tip: refer back to your SMART goal and habit you decided to build].

I will hold myself accountable by [enter all the ways you will set yourself up for success and make sure you stick to your commitment]

As I go on this journey, I will view myself as the leader of my life and choose to hold myself accountable. I will remind myself of my personal "Why" to [enter your "Why"] and will not allow myself to be swayed off the path through doubt or self-limitation. I know that I'm more than capable, and my time is now.

My [enter the name of your best self and your allies] are there to support me and I have all I need to make this goal my reality.

[Type out your name]

[Date and Signature]

Print this out and stick it on your wall so that you can see it daily. Or, have it as your screensaver, or write it into the first page of your journal. Revisit this statement when you need a reminder. Visualise how life would be if you were to achieve all of that, and think about how you feel. The more you tap into this energy, the more you will become a magnet for exactly what you want.

Three Last Tips & Tricks for Accountability

Accountability is taking responsibility for your actions and therefore, it plays a key role in self-leadership and taking ownership of your life. Including the goods and the bads. And yes, there are things that you cannot control, like which president wins the next election and them deciding to raise the taxes. But, what forever will be in your control, is dependent on how you deal with it. If you don't like the new president or the high taxes, move somewhere else. If you don't want to because all of your friends are here and you don't want to leave them behind, then focus on them and not the taxes.

Then, decide whether your love for your friends is strong enough for you to still be happy. What I want to make extra clear with this example is that taking full responsibility and accountability is not a bad thing. On the contrary, it's about you taking back your power and breaking out of any shithole that you might find yourself in. Several tools in this book will help you stay accountable, like setting goals and putting in small, consistent steps. However, I wanted to share three more with you that have helped me specifically to achieve many goals and transform my reality.

The Power of One

This is something that, as a "Manifestor" in my human design, took me a long time to learn, but also changed the game for me. My coach once said that "Being a "Manifestor "is basically ADHD but on steroids. You can sprout ideas on multiple things at once and have less tunnel vision on one thing only." And oh, how right she was. (Side note: I don't know enough about human design and the exact meanings of each type, so if you are curious, do google it). I'm really good at getting shit done. A lot of shit, to be precise. And often, also at the same time. However, when it comes to breaking through to the next level or the glass ceiling, spreading yourself very thin isn't always the best answer. Instead, you might want to try and laser-focus on one thing at a time. In business, that might be selling one offer, with one strategy on one platform at a time, and doing that consistently over time. It could also be one bold move if that is a viable option.

When it comes to designing your commitment statement, or writing out your monthly, weekly and daily goals, adopting the power of one will be of service to you as it also prevents you from overloading your plate. Another way to look at it is through setting yourself one, non-negotiable goal a day. What is one thing that you want to accomplish? Do that first, and if you have time, you can add other things, too.

Regularly Evaluate and Adjust Where Needed

You are growing and changing along the way, and regular reflection will help you to find clarity as to what action steps have been working amazingly well, and which ones didn't work as well. Notice any areas where adjustments may be necessary. Life and work circumstances change, so remain flexible and adapt your schedule and routines accordingly so that they stay in line with your goals. The same goes for your goals itself. You might find that as you are working towards them, you actually want something slightly different, or you've reached the goal but it didn't turn out exactly as planned. What helped me a lot personally was to always believe that everything is happening as it is supposed to be, or better. It's either exactly what I wanted, or better. Taking the time to reflect will reveal what has led to this and will give you the possibility to course correct. Remember to always check in with your best self and your intuition in these moments. Does it feel expansive or restrictive? Only ever go with what feels good to you.

In addition, reflecting on what worked well will show you what to continue doing or maybe even do more of. It also reveals your progress and all of the reasons to celebrate your accomplishments and lessons learned from failures. All of which are parts of growth and a necessary part of this journey you are on. This also means that there is nothing wrong with *you*. It's just how life goes, and you are doing great.

You are exactly where you are supposed to be on this journey and everything you want is possible for you.

The best way to go about this is through planning ahead when you will take the time to reflect. If you are into journaling, then this could be a shorter daily exercise. Or, you can do small rituals at the end of each month. I introduced regular mindset resets as a monthly routine, and they have been immensely helpful to not only to know what worked well and so on, but to also take time to focus on myself. I go inwards for longer than just ten to twenty minutes every day, do breathwork sessions, pull some cards, and lay new foundations with the new insights for the month ahead. Another form I highly recommend is doing a think week (or two). This is a concept I learned from Bill Gates. It basically means that you take some time offline to be with yourself at a place that cultivates calmness and focus. Whilst Gates used it to come up with new ideas, I did it to re-align with myself and my goals in life. Plus, an incredible side effect is that during this time, you will massively improve the relationship with yourself as you spend more time alone and even in silence. This led me to being a-okay with going to the cinema on my own and taking myself out for a birthday dinner. Yes, it was scary and awkward at first, but the goal is to fall in love with my own company again. Try it out and you might find that you are, in fact, a pretty cool person! Because you 100% are, my dear!

Get Yourself an Accountability Buddy

Yes, you can do everything alone. You absolutely have all that you need to become crazy successful and reach your goals and dreams. But, it's also super fun doing it with someone else. So, this is my invitation for you to drop the lone-wolf mentality and get support. One reason I became a coach is because I have a deep longing to help people. And whilst my main mission is to empower as many women as possible to eventually go their own path, one of my favourite activities is to set up accountability structures with my clients to keep them going.

The thing about motivation is that it can die quickly. Discipline, in the form of accountability, can help you keep on going, especially when others are involved. This is why I set up my group of beta-readers who are expecting a chapter from me every week. This helped me tremendously to not only reach my deadline of finishing the first manuscript, but to finish twenty-two days early. You can set up any form structures that will support you. I have had clients who paid their partners money if they didn't stick to their self-care goals. Or others chose to send me a regular update whenever they completed the task. The ones that held themselves accountable are the ones that saw the biggest impact and shift in their lives. Do make sure, when selecting an accountability buddy, that they are supportive of your dreams. We don't want any negative nellies saying, "*Ha, I told you that it's too hard. Are you sure you want to do this?*" Find the ones that cheer you on, remind yourself of your promises that uplift and challenge you when you might slip back into old habits or old ways of thinking.

Chapter Summary

In this chapter, you made a promise to yourself to stop playing small and quit watching from the side-lines only. You designed a contract that will help you stay accountable to shift your reality in the area of life that you've chosen in the beginning from its current level of satisfaction to a ten and beyond. Take it seriously because this is your *life* we are talking about right now. And you deserve to live your best life possible.

Chapter 14: The Mindset Mastery Roadmap

"The mind is everything. What you think, you become"
Buddha

Throughout this book, I have mentioned the Mindset Mastery Roadmap, which is my signature framework that I use not only when working with clients, but is how I achieved all of my own transformations thus far. With each chapter, we explored different elements of the roadmap. We dived into the power of our thoughts, because everything we do and who we are starts from within. You learned how to deal with emotions and have learned that they are merely messages that carry information about what's really going on inside of us. You now know the ins and outs about taking action, and understand the different ways to build long-lasting habits. Then, we discussed shifting your identity and explored how you see yourself in this world and ultimately, how that contributes to creating your reality.

In short, you can summarise this framework into *"Thoughts Create Reality"*. It is actually partially inspired by what Buddha once said, *"What you think you become, What you feel you attract, What you imagine you create."* (Which is also stuck as a post-it note right next to me. It's so old by now that I can barely read it, but I kept it anyway). Through my studies and work as a coach. I included the missing link of actions and habits, because there needs to be a balance between "the being" and "the doing". If you were to focus 100%

on being only, there would be no progress. If you focus solely on the doing, there would be no joy in life.

Below, you can see the framework in all of its glory. I used to have the steps on a sticky note on my wall, too. But nowadays, I don't need to be visually reminded any more, because I immediately know when my feelings are off. When I sense this, I uproot the feelings and reframe them. This takes time and practice, but is so worth it in the long run. The more you work the magic of this process, you will find yourself shifting faster and faster.

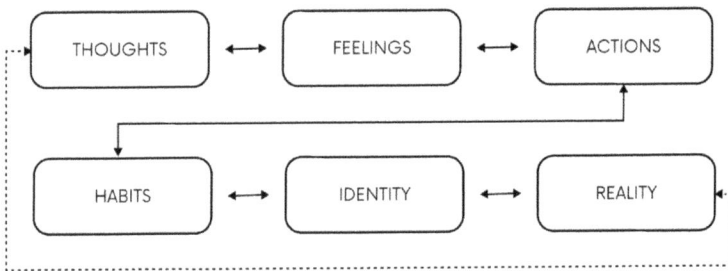

Figure: The Mindset Mastery Framework

You may notice the arrows go both ways. This is because as Antonio R. Damasio describes that: *"We are not thinking machines that feel, we are feeling machines that think."* Your emotions can therefore influence your thoughts. If you feel down, drained, and sad, your thoughts will most likely not be of a happy nature. Or, your current reality might cause you to think more negative thoughts, see yourself in a different light, and therefore might make it more challenging to work towards your goals. The power to shift things around still lies within you. This is why many people who have experienced incredible hardship, have gone on to make this world a better place. There are countless examples out there that you can take as your own proof that if you don't let life take you down, and rather see opportunity and growth in any situation, you will come out the other side better off. You will find stories of mothers who have lost their children to cancer and created charities because of it, now on a mission to save other kids' lives. You may hear stories about people who lost all mobility yet wrote best-selling books.

Focus on the fact that life happens for you.

If you are in a tough situation right now, what can you learn from this? What can you still be grateful for? Heck, what might you even be thrilled about that this is happening right now?

Whenever you do find yourself stuck in a self-limiting cycle, you can refer back to this roadmap and get yourself back on track with these supporting questions:

- *"What thoughts are coming up for me right now? Are they supportive, or not?"*

- *"How do I feel right now and what are my emotions telling me?"*

- *"What actions or inactions led to this/do I want to take?"*

- *"Are these actions habitual / what habits do I need to change?"*

- *"How do I see myself in this moment? Who do I actually want to become?"*

- *"What is my goal? How do I envision/create my dream reality?"*

You can journal your way through these, or briefly answer them in your mind whenever you catch yourself in a place you don't want to be in. Or, find your own set of questions and mini rituals that will help you use this framework whenever you want and need to. Take it, run with it, and play with it.

Here is an Example of How I Would Work Through This Framework:

I have noticed that I was struggling with receiving unconditional love from my boyfriend. The level of support that he provides me with every day when it comes to me healing, building my business, writing this book, smashing it in the gym, or just living the daily life, is on a different level. I recognised an urge within me that I always felt like I had to pay him back for it. I felt like I had to do something to fully re-tribute his love and support. I didn't allow myself to simply receive. So, I got curious as to where this limiting belief was coming from. And of course, it was derived from childhood and the experience and feeling of never being loved unconditionally. This is because I was judged, not only for things I did or didn't do, but also for just existing. It came down to the fear of being hurt by the ones I loved the most, feeling like I'm unlovable, and not deserving of being loved. None of which you can immediately tell are supportive or helpful.

This same thing goes for the emotions I was experiencing, including anger, and hurt. So, I worked the process, forgave myself for playing a part in this and forgave others for what happened. I acknowledged and released the old belief and the emotions by shifting my perspective on them. The new belief I chose was simply, "*I am worthy of being loved unconditionally*," and whenever I received something, I accepted it with gratitude and allowed myself to feel the love. If I felt the urge to make up for what I had received, I stopped for a moment and thought to myself, "*Your love as it is, is already enough.*" Don't get me wrong; this took (and still takes) conscious practice and repetition. But. it has helped increase my feelings of self-worth, joy. and my love of life (which is my number one and all-time goal). Which, in turn, changed how I see myself and my reality. I'm not second-guessing myself or what I do as much any more, and give myself grace to see when I give my best to see it as exactly that: my best.

Chapter Summary

The Mindset Mastery Roadmap is the full process and key to unlock your potential and smash through that glass ceiling that keeps you playing small. You have the tools and the power to change your life. Whatever you don't change, you choose. But let me tell you this: life is too short to keep on waking up every morning with zero joy and anticipation about the day ahead. Every day you start miserably, is one day less that you can start feeling happy. And you, my dear, deserve to be happy.

Section Summary

- Your mission statement or life purpose is what you are longing to make real in this world. It is highly aligned with your values and what lights you up, and living a life according to your statement brings fulfilment and happiness.

- The principles of stoicism are a great way to build more resilience and face life's challenges with more ease and positivity. The more you strengthen your mind to take on hardship with a good dose of positivity, the quicker you will recover and be able to move forward.

- You are your own biggest limit. Imposter syndrome, procrastination, and self-doubt can all be overcome through continuous practice. They may not ever fully disappear, and you may have moments of ups and downs. But, you know those down-moments will pass and bear their own benefits and lessons that will accelerate your journey afterwards.

- There is always more than enough for everyone. Changing your perspective from lack to abundance also means to give yourself permission to have your own full cake whilst others have their own. Another women's success story simply is proof that it is possible for you, too. If you see success all around you, it might simply mean your time is near.

- The commitment statement is a contract with yourself to continue moving forward. This statement will fuel your determination and should not be taken lightly. It is your promise towards yourself to give your dreams a fair shot. Keep your promise.

- The secret sauce to transformation and living a life you love is in the Mindset Mastery Roadmap. It's the missing aha-moment to unlock your personal next level. It also provides insight into how you got to where you are today, as well as the steps you need to take to get to where you want to be. This roadmap will help you create your dream life.

Some Last Words

First up: **WOW! You did it, girl!**

You worked through this entire book. You showed up for yourself. You discovered more about yourself, set some fire goals, decided on some inspired actions or even habits to build, and you made a promise to yourself. I'm beyond proud of you and am celebrating you like crazy right now for choosing yourself by reading this book.

You are already well on your way to playing your bigger game. You are stepping into the role of the leader of your life. No longer are you living passively. Now, you move with purpose. Come back to this book whenever you need to. It's here and it's yours. Come back to the resources whenever you yearn for additional support. But most importantly, return to yourself and your own wisdom whenever in doubt.

You know what to do. You know when you are acting from a place of alignment or misalignment. You alone have the power to make the choice. No one else can live your life for you, so take it into your own hands and become the hero of your own story. As Steve Jobbs once said:

"Your time is limited, so don't waste it by living someone else's life". Read that again.

This is your day one of your new identity and your new life. This is your day one of becoming the best version of yourself and living a life in alignment with your values. This is your day one of freeing yourself from your saboteurs and instead, fully activating your fullest potential. This is your day one of taking ownership and responsibility for the things that are inside your control. This is your day one of living life proactively and quitting the autopilot. This is day one of being full of love, gratitude, and fulfilment. This is day one of a life that will have you constantly saying, *"Fucking pinch me, I really made this happen!"*

My part in your story was to guide you to this point and to provide you with the tools so that you can go your way. It's what wizards do. They pop up when the hero is in need of guidance at the exact right time. Then, they leave when it's time for you to step up your own game. But, if you're ever in need of a wizard again, trust that you are supported, trust your own insight, seek the help, connect, and collaborate. It's so much more fun to celebrate reaching amazing goals together and to empower another. Because empowered women empower women. And you are now one of them, my dear.

Make some big shit happen and celebrate life to the max!

With love,

Josi

Gratitude

"There's always something to be grateful for."
Rhonda Byrne

I know we are coming to the end of this book. And I also know that most people might skip this part. However, I would invite you not to. Because one of the most powerful tools that will help you not only build a positive mindset, but also to shift your perspective from lack to abundance, is gratitude. In fact, having a daily gratitude practice has accompanied me throughout many years of my life. I regularly ask my incredible Insta-Family what they are grateful for in my Instagram stories. Heck, I'm even in the process of creating my very first gratitude-based journal to bring this tool to even more people out there. And I even use it to manifest.

Many people underestimate the power of gratitude, or don't see it as significant enough. Finding something to be grateful for in your darkest moments in life, might very well be the little beam of light that keeps you going. It has helped me focus on what's good in my life, even when I thought that there's nothing left. And it amplified the goodness in my life when I was overflowing with things to be grateful for. What you focus on, you grow. Being grateful for what you have doesn't stop you from creating more. On the contrary, you will attract more of what you will be grateful for. It's how this works. It's all energy. And it's a bloody high-vibe energy too!

Before we part ways, I want to share my favourite gratitude practise with you. This will surely help you upgrade your life so that you can vibe on a new level—the level of your best version of yourself.

Exercise: Manifest with Gratitude

If you already have a daily journal practice, add this exercise to it. Every day, write down a list of five to ten things that you are grateful for that are already in your life. (It doesn't matter what time of the day. I personally do it both in the morning before I start my day as well as in the evening to fall asleep with a sense of gratitude.) Then add, or sprinkle in, another five to ten things that you are grateful for that you want, but don't yet have. However, write them down in present tense, as if they're already a reality for you. This will normalise asking for and having these things in your life when they come to be, and will also get you into a visioning state. Think back to the concept I explained earlier in the book about closing the gap between where you are now and where you want to be. Being grateful now for what you have in your desired future, brings it to reality.

For example, this could look like two separate lists/paragraphs (one for what you already have, and another one for what you want): *"Today I am grateful for sipping the first Pumpkin Spice Latte of the season. I am grateful for a new ideal client signing up for a coaching program because I know this is going to be life changing for her. I am grateful for the extra cuddles with my cat.*

I am grateful for waking up to the soft sound of waves crashing at the beach in front of my house. I'm grateful for reaching best-selling status with my books. I'm grateful for our two little wonderful kids that are playing in the sand right now building sandcastles."

Try it out for at least thirty days and see how it goes for you as you work towards your goals. If you want to take it up a notch, also take some time to feel the gratitude. For me, this shows up as an expansive feeling in my chest. I get excited and experience a feeling of deep love for life. For you, it might be different. It could be super energising, or ground and calm you. The importance is to tune into it, and allow yourself to be fully bathed in this sensation of gratitude. That's how you will get into this high-vibe state, and where magic happens. If you sense any negative emotions, or your saboteurs are saying, *"Hi, hello, you can't have that because of X reason"*, then that's awesome! You just shed light on another limiting belief that you can shift and release to call in what you deserve.

Acknowledgements

And with this, I want to express some words of gratitude for everyone that has helped me on this journey to fulfil my childhood dream and become an author. This book has been waiting within me for so many years. Yet, I'm glad it did wait because I could infuse it with so much more life lessons, transformations, and pour my whole obsession about mindset and coaching into it. And, as we are talking about our best versions of ourselves, I have to thank myself for bringing this book into reality. I'm grateful to have taken the steps and have sat down every workday to write these pages. Whilst I'm typing this, I hear the famous speech from Snoop Dog in my head, which he starts off with "*I wanna thank me (...)*". The thing is, he is right! We got to acknowledge our own hard work and celebrate ourselves and our accomplishments first and foremost. If we don't claim our own brilliance, we give it away, and that's not what I wanted to achieve with this book. And I'm fucking chuffed that I finally did it! Not only that, but the first manuscript of this book took me way less time than I thought it would. Of course, including the edits and getting to my second and third draft added some time to it. However, the essence of this book has been waiting within me for so long, poured into the keyboard and onto this Google Document in under three months. Literally, I'm mind-blown!

What's also mind-blowing is *you*, my dear reader! I, of course, also want to thank you, but besides that, I invite you to thank yourself for letting me be part of your life's journey. Take a moment to thank yourself for finishing the book, for doing the exercises, and for committing to yourself. This is *huge*! So many people might not even get to this point or level of self-awareness in this lifetime. But you did. You kept an open mind. You were willing to evolve and to look at yourself and life from a new perspective. You claimed ownership over your life, and you learned to trust your own power. This deserves a standing ovation!!! You are flipping amazing, girl. Keep on going, I believe in you!

Next up, I've got to say thanks to my boyfriend and ride or die for always supporting me and respecting my writing hours. (I literally banned him from the room from ten to eleven). I'm grateful for him for always listening to me ramble about my book, asking me insightful questions that helped me make this book even better, and for celebrating every word count milestone with me. But also, for telling me off when I got too invested or worked up. He never failed to remind me to take a break and chillax. Never have I ever experienced such genuine, deep support, and love before. And whilst I know I could have done it all alone, I'm glad I didn't have to.

Which brings me to my amazing beta readers and my editor. You have been with me on the journey of completing my first manuscript and were a vital part to bringing this book to live. Knowing you will expect a new chapter every week to read through and comment on, helped me tremendously to keep up to my word and keep on going. Your comments, questions, reactions, edits (especially when it came to commas because they are clearly not my forte), and feedback helped me to have a strong first manuscript that then evolved into this final version of the book I'm so proud of.

Thank you!

Additional Resources

Who doesn't love some extra resources that can make their life easier?! Exactly, no one!

To access all the resources that come with this book, copy and paste the link below into your browser of choice and enter the code: "HERWAY"- www.josidumont.com/herway. On this page, you will find the following resources that you have lifetime access to:

Chapter 1: The Wheel of Life Template

Chapter 2: Quiz: Find out Your Self-Sabotage Type

Chapter 3: Mood-Tracker Template

Chapter 4: Meditation "A Journey Into the Past"

Chapter 4: Rewrite Your Limiting Beliefs Template

Chapter 5: Walking Meditation "5-4-3-2-1"

Chapter 7: Meditation "Activate Your Best Self"

Chapter 7: Meditation "Channel Your Allies or Best Self"

Chapter 7: Round-table Exercise Template

Chapter 9: Habit Workbook

Chapter 13: Commitment Statement Template

Next Steps

If you loved this book and are interested in any of my coaching programs or courses, head over to josidumont.com. Also, make sure to sign up to my weekly newsletter "Wisdom Bites" for regular goodies and news. But most importantly, do connect with me on Instagram @josi_dumont. I would love to hear your thoughts on this book and to cheer you on as you reach your goals.

References

- Martin R. Huecker; Jacob Shreffler; Patrick T. McKeny; David Davis (2023, July 31). *Imposter phenomenon.* StatPearls

- Vinoth K. Ranganathan, Vlodek Siemionow, Jing Z. Liu, Vinod Sahgal, Guang H. Yue, *From mental power to muscle power—gaining strength by using the mind*, Neuropsychologia, Volume 42, Issue 7, (2004)

- Wheel of Emotions Graph, Geoffrey Roberts; https://imgur.com/gallery/tCWChf6

Other useful books mentioned and that I would recommend:

- Gary Vaynerchuk (2021): *"Twelve and a Half"*

- James Clear (2018): *"Atomic Habits"*

- *Simon Sinek (2011): "Start With Why"*

- Mel Robbins (2017): *"The Five Second Rule"*

- William B. Irvine (2019): *"The Stoic Challenge"*

- *Rhonda Byrne (2006): "The Secret"*

9 798224 102105